Betty

A Story
of Courage and Love

A Story
of Courage and Love

Arland O. Fiske

Til Oliver og Jean —

Hilsen fra
Arland Fiske
8-14-04
Fiskehaven

North American Heritage Press

Copyright © MCMXCVIII
by Arland O. Fiske

For permissions, or for serialization, condensation, or for adaptations, write the Author at HCR 70, Box 649A, Laporte, MN 56461, USA.

International Standard Book Number: 0-942323-30-0
Library of Congress Catalog Card Number 98-67831

Published by
North American Heritage Press
A DIVISION OF
CREATIVE MEDIA, INC.
P.O. Box 1
Minot, North Dakota 58702, USA
701/852-5552

Printed in the United States of America

FOREWORD

ELL-NOTED FOR HIS EFFORTS at researching and bringing alive the important cultural history and rich traditions of Scandinavians through his short stories, Arland Fiske uses his talents to bring life to World War II Denmark through the real-life eyes of Betty Poulson and Erik Waehrens in *Betty: A Story of Courage and Love*. It personalizes the hardships of the Danish people during the Nazi reign, winding a love story with well-rounded historical research – which is obviously Fiske's labor of love.

Telling the story of Betty allowed Fiske to try something different – use his extensive research skills about Scandinavia and compose a novelette in the form of a docudrama, which The Pioneer and others ran in a 32-part serialization. The author of several books on Scandinavian history and lore, Fiske wanted to try his hand at relating what is essentially a true story, molded with the historical background of the Danish people during the trying times of the rise of Hitler, the German occupation of Denmark and of the Danish Resistance movement. It also allowed the newspaper to bring back a reader service from a bygone era – the serialization of a story from week-to-week in our daily newspaper. The story becomes even more valuable in our northern Minnesota area, rich in Scandinavian history and parentage.

The grandson of Norwegian and Danish immigrants myself, I yearn for information about my heritage. I followed Betty's travels across the Atlantic Ocean to a country of which she knew little of, thinking my grandparents must have had the same thought as they ventured across the ocean decades earlier from Copenhagen and from a small fishing village on the northwest coast of Norway. Only this time, Betty and Erik also had to contend with a major world war and we learn not only of their personal story, but, also of the great efforts of the Danish people in coping with perhaps the darkest times of this century.

As in all his work – in books and in weekly newspaper columns – Fiske's goal is to keep the past alive for those of Scandinavian heritage, that we not forget the people, places, events and legends that shape our history, culture and traditions. He and his wife, Gerda, now live near Laporte, south of Bemidji, and his stories have made us richer in understanding our Scandinavian heritage.

It is through Fiske's painstaking efforts and attention to detail that a period of Scandinavian history – of my heritage – can be personalized and brought to life. While it tells the story of Betty and Erik, it reflects the story of many Danish couples and the unselfish courage they displayed during a dark time. Many of us can relate to that story in our own backgrounds, and now begin to understand what it is that shapes us as Scandinavians.

As a people, we prepare for the future by learning of our past. For those of us who are proud to call Norway, Denmark, Sweden, Finland or Iceland our homeland, we thank Arland Fiske for giving us that insight.

– *Brad Swenson*
Managing Editor
The Pioneer
Bemidji, Minn.

PREFACE

I FIRST MET BETTY and her husband, Erik Waehrens, at our wedding in August 1952, in Racine, Wisconsin. They had moved to America with the thought that if all went well they may perhaps make it their permanent home. I met them again in January 1953, when they were about to return to Denmark.

In July 1977, we visited them at their home in Bindslev, Denmark, and spent several pleasant days as their guests. It was during that time the idea of writing this story surfaced, at the suggestion of my wife, Gerda. Gerda's father and Betty's mother were brother and sister. Upon our return to America, I began gathering information for the story. However, due to many reasons, professional and personal, the book never came to be. In September 1985, we visited them again at their home in Bindslev and spent several more delightful days as their guests. Additional information was gathered for writing their story. But again, the story was not written.

In the meantime, I wrote and published seven books of Scandinavian stories, including stories about Denmark. It was only after retirement from pastoral ministry that there was afforded the time to do the extensive reading necessary for capturing the setting of their story. So finally, after twenty years, the story has been written.

While this is a true story, there are a few incidents where it was necessary to employ some fiction to tie the story together with conversation. But even where this was necessary, earnest attempt was made to make these lines correspond to what I knew to be true of them and their times. All references to the world scene, including World War II, can be historically documented.

The subtitle of this book is called *A Story of Courage and Love*. The word courage is derived from the Greek word "kardia," translated "heart." It means daring to move ahead even when afraid. By the strange evolution of language this word arrived into the English vocabulary through the Norman Conquest of England in 1066. Incidentally, many of these French-speaking Normans (Northmen) had Danish ancestry. The word expresses the feelings of resolution and tenacity.

"Love" is the most misunderstood word in the English language. Love, as used in this title, is almost synonymous with courage, for they are both actions of the heart. Both Betty and Erik were gifted with these powers for living.

I was challenged to write this story because it's an account of two gracious people and their family which, in my opinion, should be told for its own sake and for the human values which their lives have exhibited. To write this story has been a privilege as well as a work of love. I am much indebted to Betty and Erik Waehrens for their willingness to share their life's story for publication.

This book could not have been completed without the help of my wife, Gerda, who has assisted in editing all my books. It was her idea that the story should be written and that I should do it. I am also indebted to Jill Schlictling of the Pilot-Independent newspaper in Walker, Minnesota, for her editorial assistance. I am privileged to have had Dr. Sidney A. Rand, former president of St. Olaf College, Northfield, Minnesota, and ambassador to Norway, read and critique the manuscript. The shortcomings of the manuscript, however, are my own responsibility.

I am grateful to the editors of the Minot Daily News in North Dakota, the Bemidji Pioneer and the Pilot-Independent of Walker, both in Minnesota, for their willingness to serialize the story for their readers. This has given me the benefit of reader response and to make needed corrections in the manuscripts.

I continue to be deeply indebted to Allen O. Larson and the North American Heritage Press for publishing this my eighth volume of Scandinavian stories, and to Sheldon Larson for designing the cover. Without the special interest in my writing by them, these volumes would probably never have been possible.

I am also indebted to many other people and sources, too numerous to mention. My hope is that something of Betty and Erik's quiet courage and love may touch the hearts of those who read their story.

Betty and Erik continue to make their home in Bindslev, a community which they love and where they are loved. Bindslev is a quaint little city near the North Sea. May their kind of people live forever! The world needs more people like them.

– Arland O. Fiske
Kabekona Lake
Laporte, Minnesota
September 2*, 1998

* *Remembrance Day for Nikolai Frederik Severin Grundtvig (1783-1872), Bishop, hymnwriter, educator and renewer of the Danish Church.*

PUBLICATIONS
BY ARLAND O. FISKE

The Scandinavian Heritage Series:

The Scandinavian Heritage

The Scandinavian World

The Scandinavian Spirit

The Scandinavian Adventure

The Scandinavian Heritage
Audio Cassette
(Twelve Stories From *The Scandinavian Heritage* Book)

❧

The Best of
The Norwegian Heritage

Stories from
The Swedish Heritage

The Best of
The Norwegian Heritage, Volume II

Betty: A Story of Courage and Love

Contents

CHAPTER 1

A Small Town In Jutland

THERE'S A SMALL TOWN in the very north of Denmark named Bindslev, which the Danes pronounce "BIN-sloo." It's just a few miles from the North Sea where the Skagerrak and the Kattegat meet as clashing seas. Everything else appears tranquil, as calm and peaceful as a storybook tale. In fact, to a visitor from the bustling centers of the world with their junk yards of old automobiles, smog-filled air and wide super-highways, Denmark looks like a doll's house. The yards are neatly kept, the fields are planted next to the roads, and everything seems to be in its proper place.

That's the way Bindslev and Vendsyssel, the entire area north of the Limfjord, looked until April 9, 1940. On that fateful day the bitter years began. The Wehrmacht, the Nazi war machine, came storming into Denmark. Within a few hours this once peace-loving nation became a prison for its people and its resources were plundered by an enemy which professed to be a friend. Seventy-six years of peace were shattered in one night while the people slept. The morning brought a rude awakening.

Nor was Denmark the only country to feel the fury of Hitler's deceptive madness. Norway fell the same day. The Norwegians fought a fierce rear guard battle until the king and his cabinet were safely evacuated to England. Active resistance continued "underground" until Germany surrendered, May 4, 1945. The nightmare had lasted for five years. Fortunately, Denmark and Norway did not experience the devastation of Poland, just seven months before.

But the Lowlands, Belgium and the Netherlands, were overrun less than two months later. The proud armies of France, victorious over their enemy just two decades before, were smashed, suffering an inglorious defeat as the Wehrmacht rolled on. Great Britain and its far-flung empire stood alone in their unreadiness for the days of darkness which were soon to cover the earth.

Back in Bindslev, Erik Waehrens was waiting for word from his fiancee in America. He had written a proposal of marriage and she had promised to return to her homeland. That had been two years before when there still seemed to be hope that war could be averted. After all, Britain's Prime Minister, Neville Chamberlain, had returned from a meeting on September 30, 1938, with Hitler in Munich with the assuring words, "There will be peace in our time." It would be safe for Betty to return.

In the aftermath of the great depression which struck Denmark as well as America, wages were low. It had taken the combined earning efforts of both Erik and Betty to save enough for her return trip to Denmark. Why hadn't he heard something? Had she changed her mind? America was still a nation at peace. Perhaps her family in America had convinced her to wait until the war was over. His heart beat heavily.

The oddsmakers were betting on Hitler to win the war. England alone held out with hope, but the people were losing confidence in their leaders. One voice had been calling for England to rearm and to gird itself for battle – Winston Churchill's. But at the war's outbreak, his was a "voice crying in the wilderness." The leaders who were guiding the nation were still hoping against hope. Number 10 Downing Street didn't seem to have the right stuff to rouse the people.

It's not strange then that there were many who decided the better part of wisdom was to side with the apparent victors. One couldn't know whom to trust any more. Even old friends might be secretly collaborating with the enemy. It seemed to many people that the king, the parliament, the military, and the police, had decided to cooperate with the enemy.

Erik was troubled. He was a patient person by nature and was not one to show his deepest emotions. But those about him knew the anxiety burning in his soul. Was his dream for Betty's return to be destroyed like his country's freedom? He would wait – what else could he do? He would have to remain in Bindslev while the German soldiers passed through his town to their fortifications on the North Sea. The days were becoming bitter.

Betty — A Story Of Courage And Love

CHAPTER 2

An Unlikely Surprise

SENIUS LANGLOKKEN WAS A SEA CAPTAIN who had returned to retire in his native Bindslev in Denmark. He had been around the world many times and had many narrow escapes, but never lost a ship. Old age was catching up to him. He retired shortly before the outbreak of World War II in September 1939. Now he would wait out his days in the little village by the North Sea. Senius, however, still had a keen eye for world events and was an avid newspaper reader. His sailing friends picked up newspapers for him wherever they put into port. He especially liked America. A New York newspaper could make him forget his arthritis and rheumatic pains, not to mention the evil days that had befallen his homeland since April 9, 1940.

In the Waehrens clothing store in Bindslev, Kaj (pronounced "Kai"), Erik's oldest brother in a family of ten, had overheard Senius tell his father about a newspaper delivered to him from New York. The newspaper was two weeks old, not so bad for those days when the Nazis censored all mail, causing delay in delivery. On the front page of the New York Times there was a picture of Betty holding Erik's photograph. She was about to return to Bindslev for her wedding.

Kaj was frantically looking for Erik, though he dare not reveal his haste lest a collaborator report him to the Nazis. Erik was busy doing tailoring in his father's business. He had been deep in thought when Kaj found him. He was worried about Betty. He'd sent her money for the Pan Am Clipper flight. Had she gotten the required visas? Would the Germans give her passage from Berlin when their transportation system was severely tested by the war?

"Yes, what is it? You have some news?" Erik was almost afraid to ask, "Is it about Betty?" "Listen," said Kaj, "do you remember Senius Langlokken, the old sea captain born in Bindslev? He doesn't get around much any more but he has connections. I heard him tell Peder Bock and Father that Betty is already on her way to Denmark. He has a newspaper from New York with her picture!"

It was only a short distance from the Waehrens house to the city square where the Saturday morning open market was in progress. Farmers brought in their garden vegetables, eggs, cream, and fresh meat to sell. German soldiers would come all the way from Frederikshavn and were often their best customers. They had more money then the Danes. There was fresh fish, too, but not like it had been in the days before the occupation. Now the Danish fishermen had to obtain a special permit from their "deliverers" to take their boats out to net fish. The watchful eyes of the German guns in the bunkers on the beach and on coast guard ships restricted their fishing. Yet, the Germans realized they needed food, too. So carefully instructed fishermen were given permission, but only with German guards on board.

By the time Erik and Kaj arrived, Senius was nowhere to be found. He had been last seen walking over the bridge to the south of the business section. Walking as fast as they dared, so as not to attract attention, they headed for the bridge. Though German troops were not quartered in Bindslev at the time, the enemy's presence was felt everywhere. It was to be assumed that spies and paid informers might be most anywhere. They could hardly keep from running, but they thought better of it. As they approached the bridge, they met Jens Clausen. "Herr Clausen, have you seen Captain Langlokken? We heard that he was going towards the bridge."

Jens was a much wiser man than most people would have guessed. Behind those dull, gray eyes and grisly beard was a mind that didn't miss a nuance. It was suspected that Jens might be pretty high up in the Danish Underground, but so far, the Germans did not seem to have caught on to him. Jens had known John Waehrens, Erik's father, from childhood. "What do you want with the Captain, my boys?" Jens spoke with an air of innocence. Kaj explained their excitement. "I think you may find him with Lars Larsen, but you better not waste any time. You can never depend on finding old sailors when you want them."

Erik and Kaj walked swiftly to the Larsen place. It was on the edge of the village and there was a small chicken coop and a stable attached to the house. At their approach the dog barked and the geese began to flap their wings. Erik opened the gate and called out, "Captain Langlokken, are you here?" Presently, the old sea captain appeared. His beard was white. So were his bushy eye brows. He wore the typical sea captain's cap not so different from those worn in far away Greece.

"What do you want?" the captain asked. Kaj, being older, had casually met the old captain at the Waehrens store, but Erik had not. "Captain Langlokken," Kaj said, "This is my brother Erik. It is his intended who is returning to Denmark. We heard that you had some news. Do you have the newspaper here with the picture?" Senius treasured his newspapers from abroad. He'd paid a good price for their delivery, so he never let one get out of his hands until he was totally through with it.

"So you are Erik," he said. "I'm glad to meet you. Yes, I received a New York Times from Captain Bensen. His ship, the Dansk Prinz, arrived in Frederikshavn just two days ago. The paper is already two weeks old now, but that is not so bad these days. Come inside and I'll show it to you." They went into the house through the back door. It was a low cottage, but well enough kept. It was cozy, but not well, lighted. Kerosene was hard to come by those days.

Erik was so excited that his pulse could be heard in his own ears. Slowly the old captain dug the paper out from his grip. "Here," he said, "is your Betty." There she was, getting ready to fly from New York to Copenhagen (spelled Kobenhavn in Danish and pronounced "kOOB-enhauen"). At first, Erik was all joy. Then he grew numb and pale. An awesome feeling began to paralyze all his reflexes. "If Betty left over two weeks ago, why hasn't she arrived? Has something gone wrong?" These were his fearful thoughts. He could say no more. He was sure that the worst had happened. Had the plane gone down at sea, perhaps in a storm? Was Betty a prisoner of the Nazis? Did they think that she was a spy? Guilt covered his heart like a funeral pall. "Why did I ever ask her to leave Racine," he mumbled. "She would have been much safer with her family in Wisconsin."

Alone In Manhattan

"DEAR LORD, HELP ME! What will I do? Why has this terrible thing happened to me? I'm so afraid!" Betty was alone in the Metro Hotel just off 43rd Street in Manhattan. She had arrived in New York the day before from Chicago. By this time she had expected to be over the Atlantic flying home to Denmark. It was not until she had arrived in New York that the bad news hit her. A Portuguese and a Spanish visa would be needed for the trip home, as well as British and German visas. The travel agency in Chicago had not told her this. There would be a two-week delay. As it was, Betty had scraped together as much money as she could just to make the trip. Besides the living costs in New York City, the ticket would cost a hundred dollars more due to the delay.

It seemed needlessly cruel. All her life, Betty had felt herself dangling between newly-found joys and crushed hopes. On the first day away from Wisconsin, she cried her heart out on the hotel bed. What could she do besides cry?

Betty's mind was in a whirl with the recent events. There was the trip from Racine to Midway Airport on Chicago's southwest side. It had been a hard farewell. Her family pleaded with her to wait until the war might be over. Perhaps it would not last too long and things would become normal again. One good thing, America was neutral, though supplying arms to Great Britain. Maybe the Red Cross could arrange for Erik to come to Racine.

Courage came to Betty in those long moments of parting because she was in love. Deep within herself she felt that this trip was the Lord's will for her and Erik. It didn't matter that it may be difficult. But all her obstacles were in America, not in Denmark. She saw a Gideon Bible on the dresser and decided to read. She found Psalm 103 and hoped that it would speak to her:

"As a father pitieth his children,

So the Lord pitieth those who fear him."

She started to pull herself together and remembered that there was an address of a girl friend's friend packed away in her suitcase. She had met Kathie Jensen at night school while learning English. Kathie tried to meet every newcomer from Denmark. Perhaps one of them might know her orphaned cousins who lived in Abenra, a port city in the south of Jutland, near the border of Germany by Flensborg. No such luck. Betty was from Bindslev up by the North Sea. Still, they remained good friends, sharing their dreams and tears.

When Kathie learned that Betty was to go through New York and have an overnight stay, she immediately thought of her friend, Inger Olsen. "I want to give you the address of my friend Inger. Please call her when you get to New York, if you have time," Kathie said with her infectious enthusiasm. Inger had been special to Kathie since she had come from Vejle, not far north of Abenra. She had not known Kathie's cousins, but just being from a nearby city made them feel close to each other.

Inger had been engaged to a Polish boy. But just before the wedding, he left her without a word. She learned that he had been living with a waitress in Milwaukee during the week while working there. The word was that the other girl's priest had arranged a confrontation. There was no fight. Inger was too embarrassed to stay any longer in Racine, so she decided to go to New York where there lived some other Danish friends who had come to America. After being without work for three weeks, she finally got a job at Macy's as a clerk in the women's wear department. She had a special talent as a seamstress and had some abilities at designing women's apparel. The "Garment District" of Manhattan was a good place to get over her heart break in the Midwest. Besides that, Inger used to sew all her own clothes.

Betty frantically searched her bags. Where was the address? It always happens that way. When you get excited, you can't see what's right in front of you. Here was Kathie's note: "Betty, when you get to New York, please try to call my friend Inger. She is now Mrs. Helmut Zorn and lives at 1879 8th Street, Bronx, New York." Betty decided that she must call at once. Her money was limited and $6.00 a day for the hotel plus the cost of meals was beyond Betty's budget for two weeks. She found the number in the phone book and it matched the number given by Kathie.

"Operator, please call 614-2218. Yes, this is room 407. Yes, I'm Miss Poulson, the one who checked in yesterday. No, I won't be able to leave today. My flight has been delayed." The phone continued to ring. Finally, the operator broke in to say:

"I'm sorry, your party does not answer. I suggest that you call later. Perhaps your party is at work."

Betty tried again, six times and still no answer. She didn't know whether to cry or to get angry. Her eye caught a worn yellow card on the mirror of the dresser: "Go Western Union. Send your message by telegram." She rang the number and gave this message: "Friend of Kathie Jensen. Need help. Please call 471-6200, Room 407. Betty Poulson." It was already late on Friday and the telegram was not delivered until the next morning. But no phone call answered her plea. Betty spent the weekend alone, the loneliest weekend of her life.

CHAPTER 4

A Friend In Need

*D*URING THAT LONG AND LONELY WEEKEND in a Manhattan hotel, Betty kept waiting for Inger to call her. Inger and her husband Helmut, however, had gone out of the city to visit friends. These friends were Swedes and not Danes, but at least they could talk to each other in a language which came directly from the heart. Helmut was a German from Slesvig, where many Danes lived. He understood their language and had often sailed his boat in Danish waters, having travelled to the Vejle Fjord

Inger first met Helmut when he had come to Macy's to buy a woolen sweater for his mother on her birthday. He had noticed her accent. It was not hard for them to become good friends. That had been in May. There were married in September.

Inger and Helmut were very tired after their weekend trip up the Hudson River so they never noticed the telegram in the mailbox until Monday morning. Inger read the message and immediately placed a call to Betty. The phone rang only once. "Hello, yes, this is Betty Poulson. I'm so glad to hear your voice. I've tried all weekend to reach you. I almost gave up. You don't know me, but I'm a friend of Kathie Jensen. She asked me to greet you from her and said that if needed any help in New York I could call you." Betty told Kathie her story. Inger replied: "I've got a week of vacation. I'll be over to the Metro just as soon as I can get my things together. You can stay at my house until your travel plans are straightened out."

Hanging up the phone Betty fell on her bed, sobbing tears of relief. The words of Psalm 103 welled up within her:

"Bless the Lord, O my soul

and all that is within me,

bless his holy name."

There was more fear than pure joy in Betty's soul, but at least she now felt safe.

Inger came to the Metro and Betty was off on her first subway ride. Arriving at Inger's home in the Bronx, she was treated to the most welcome ableskiver dinner that she had ever eaten.

"Now, let's talk about your plans. How are we going to get you to Denmark? I know a girl who works at a travel bureau. Maybe she can help." That's what Betty had asked for – help.

When first arriving in New York, Betty had gone to the Spanish Embassy. They said that there would be no problem getting a visa. But the staff person was not helpful when he said: "Don't go. He is probably married to somebody else by now." Betty was hurt by the words because she knew in her heart that Erik would never do a thing like what happened to Inger.

The Portuguese Embassy was something else. "Yes, Miss Poulson, you can get a visa, but it will take two weeks. Things take more time these days." So Inger took Betty to the Midtown Travel Bureau. That's where Margie, Inger's friend, proved helpful. "I'm awfully sorry, Betty, about your having to pay a hundred dollars more for your ticket. But why don't you write a letter to the President of Pan Am explaining your situation. It's worth a try. I've heard of it done before." Betty wrote, appealing to his feelings, as Margie suggested. It worked. Three days later a phone call came from the president's office asking for Betty. The extra fee was waived. Something had gone right!

Betty stayed a week in the Bronx at Inger's home. But since Inger was going back to work the following Monday and there would be nothing to do, she called her Uncle Martin in Albany. "Sure, you can come to visit us. We'd love to see you." Betty took the bus upstate were she stayed almost a week. Lots of tears and hugs were shared as Betty boarded the bus again for New York.

Betty was now on her own to ride the subways. She became hopelessly lost. Shaking all over, she found a policeman who helped her to find a phone. Once again, Inger came to the rescue. When Betty finally left New York, she lost all contact with her friend in the Bronx. When war broke out between America and Germany, Betty was cut off from the New World in the West. She kept hoping that perhaps the Red Cross would get a message to Inger.

BETTY — A STORY OF COURAGE AND LOVE

CHAPTER 5

A Little Girl Again

*D*URING THAT LONESOME LAST NIGHT in New York, Betty had a lot of time to think. Suddenly, she was a twelve-year-old girl again. It was like a psychic earthquake. The ground under her feet was shaken. Up until that day, Betty had been happy and secure with her grandparents in Denmark.

"Betty, I think maybe you should go to live with your mother in America." As the words sank in, Betty was stunned. She ran to her grandmother, threw her arms about her, protesting: "But Grandma, you are the only mother I've ever had. I don't ever want to leave you."

Grandma knew better, but her tears agreed with Betty. "Grandpa is not well. He may not have long to live," she said, trying to console Betty's fears. She also knew that Betty had to go out into the world like her own children had done. Some had gone to America and some found homes for themselves in Denmark. They talked some more.

"But Grandma, what will happen to me if you die before I can go to my mother?" Aunt Margrethe, sister to Betty's mother, was visiting when grandma talked to Betty. "Dear Betty, you can come and stay with us, if Grandma dies." Betty's fear and sorrow lifted. Suddenly, she was happy again, like only little girls can experience it. Betty's thoughts that night were all about America, that wonderful new land across the sea. It was so far away and it must be so big.

Living up on the far north tip of the Jutland peninsula, Betty had seen many large ocean liners. Some docked in the port at Frederikshavn. Many sailed by and went to Copenhagen or Gothenburg in Sweden. Others went to Oslo in Norway. She supposed that some must go to America, too. Wisconsin must be a real place and not just make-believe since some of her uncles, aunts, cousins, and friends had come back to visit. Even Grandpa had left Grandma one summer to work on a farm in Minnesota while visiting his family in America. He had told so many stories about it.

Denmark was just a little country compared to America. Land was precious in Denmark. There were no junk yards, not even ditches separating the fields from the roads. The air was clean, no dust storms like there were in America during the Thirties. Clean dairy farms were nestled in the gently-rolling countrysides. Grass grew everywhere, except on the sand dunes by the ocean beaches.

As Betty waited for the morning and the Clipper trip back to Denmark, she thought of the brave Vikings who once inhabited her homeland. She remembered that not far away on the heights above the Limfjord by Norresunby, there were ruins of a large Viking winter camp. There they prepared for raids on England in the following summer. It's peaceful there today, just some unclaimed sheep grazing where warriors once camped in winter. In those days, Denmark was feared everywhere. Its warriors pillaged at will over England, Normandy, parts of Norway, Sweden, islands of the North Sea, and the coastal areas on the Baltic. Even parts of Ireland had once been ruled by Vikings.

Denmark was different now. Since the conversion of Denmark from the worship of Odin, Thor and Frey to the God of the Christians, they began to lose their dedication to battle. It didn't happen quickly. It had been 950 years since St. Ansgar and other missionaries had won the day for the teacher from Nazareth. Many battles had been fought in Jutland by those legendary warriors. The government has marked many of the ancient military encampments as places to be remembered. The love of battle, including human sacrifice to appease the gods, had ceased. Denmark was a land at peace with its neighbors. The only wars were those within the heart, like the one struggling to surface in Betty's soul.

Alone in her room that night, the house being dark and silent, Betty wondered: "Will my mother be glad to see me when I get to America?"

CHAPTER 6

Light From The Past

$\mathcal{A}$ WEEK WENT BY and Aunt Margrethe came to visit Grandma again. Grandpa seemed to be a little better. Grandma knew, however, that she might soon be alone. He was getting weaker.

Questions, unasked before, now refused to be quiet any longer. "Grandma, tell me about my mother." Grandma drew Betty close to her side. Betty could hardly wait.

"Your mother was a sweet and quiet girl. She loved to go out in the fields to take care of the sheep and even when there was lightning and thunder, she was not afraid." She added this, of course, because Betty was so easily frightened by such things.

"When your mother was thirteen, she began to work on a farm. Then she would come home for a while in between jobs. But as usual for girls in the early 1900s, she worked on many farms for several years. In many cases, their wages were sent home to support their families.

"On one of these farms, she met a young man who said he loved her. She thought she loved him, too. When she came

21

home to visit once, I knew something was wrong. We both cried and cried together. The young man wanted to marry her, but Grandpa said: "No, she is promised to John." John had already gone to America to find a job. Later, he had told Grandpa that he would send for her.

Betty's mother and John had known each other from childhood. They had become close friends and John dreamed of marrying her some day. And even after his dream girl's tragedy, he still wanted her to be his wife.

A few weeks later, Aunt Margrethe told her more. It had been a tragedy for the family. Betty's mother was no longer the carefree and happy girl she had once been. She could not understand why it had happened.

"When you were born," Aunt Margrethe continued, "your mother worried so much about you." 'How can I take care of her?' she would ask Grandma. It was agreed. Your mother would go to America. John still wanted her to come. He would marry her and when they saved up enough money to have you with them, some one would bring you to them."

"Auntie," Betty tried hard to say, "Do you think my mother will know me when she sees me? I'm a big girl now. Will her other children like me? Does John still want me to come?"

Life in America did not bring swift riches to John and his new family. He worked hard to secure a home and support them. Fortunately, Racine, Wisconsin, was a city to which many Danish people had immigrated. For many years, it was known as the most Danish city in America. As more of his countrymen settled in the community, Danish churches were built. They were also social centers where the young unmarried immigrants could meet. Dania, a Danish club was organized where friends could gather to share news from their homeland and tell each other about where good jobs could be found. It was a place where excellent Danish meals were served. The Danish Brotherhood also had programs and parties for the immigrants from the "Old Country."

Racine was becoming an industrial city with many job opportunities. It was already famous for building sturdy farm wagons. Danish businesses were established, especially bakeries, where the immigrants could buy their favorite breads and pastries. It helped them to feel "at home" in this new and wonderful land of opportunity. So when the word circulated back in Denmark about where was the best place in America to go to, Racine became widely-known.

As it happened, no money came from America to bring Betty to her mother. The worldwide depression of the 1930s had also come to Racine. Betty would be one more mouth to feed in her mother's growing family. Besides that, Grandma and Grandpa wanted to keep Betty as long as they could. She had become like their own child to them. Betty was not unaware of their deep feelings for her. Those are not unnatural feelings for grandparents.

The conversation of the day thundered in Betty's mind that night. She was torn between wanting to be with her mother in America and staying with her grandparents in Denmark. These were flashes of light on her hidden past. Betty hardly saw and heard the violent storm that had rolled in from the sea as the sun set.

As sleep came to Betty's tired spirit, she wondered: "Why am I so different from all my friends?"

CHAPTER 7

Back In School

"GRANDMA, GRANDMA, WHERE ARE YOU?" It was still dark outside as Betty turned restlessly. Then she realized that she was still in New York at Inger's house. But Grandma had seemed so real and Aunt Margrethe, too.

It was deathly quiet and soon Betty was feeling very sleepy again. A strange thing happened. Here it was in late August and a Christmas carol was floating through Betty's mind. At times like these, sounds and pictures pass through one's consciousness quickly. There she saw him. It was Herr Nels Christiansen, her school teacher in Bindslev. She was happy again. He had a way of making school fun, especially during music class.

There it came again: *"Deilig er den Himmel bla..."*

> *"Bright and glorious is the sky,*
>
> *radiant are the heavens high,*
>
> *Where the golden stars are shining,*
>
> *all their rays to earth inclining.*
>
> *Beckoning us to heaven above,*
>
> *beckoning us to heaven above."*

Once more, Betty was sound asleep. Neither the war across the sea nor the busyness of America's greatest metropolis could crowd out the happy feelings that Betty had about herself.

In a little while she was back at Grandpa's farm, just a short distance northwest of the village. She felt safe and happy. There was the school building. And there was Herr Christiansen, too, saying, "Good morning, children. I'm glad to see you." As they began their day of instruction, he would read from the Bible and say a prayer for everyone in school. He would always remember those who were absent and those whose families had illness. He had remembered Grandpa many times, too. Then would come classes in reading, arithmetic, history (especially of Denmark), writing, Bible stories, and singing. Music was the best one of all. Herr Christiansen made all the songs sound so beautiful.

One day he looked at Betty and said: "Betty, is there something wrong?" "Yes, Herr Christiansen, my grandmother is not feeling well. She is so pale and weak, and just can't keep warm." The good teacher walked to her desk and said, "Today, we will all pray for your grandmother." Betty could not hold back her tears, but she felt better.

School might have been a paradise except for Arne Clausen. He was a nasty tease and would pull her braids. Even now, she wanted to scream at him, "Leave me alone, you old meanie!" Arne was careful not to bother Betty whenever Herr Christiansen was near. So Betty would often offer to help her teacher if it was one of Arne's bad days.

Betty remembered that Grandpa didn't have much money, but Grandma always had food for the table, even when company would come. Grandma also always had clean clothes for Betty to wear to school every day. Many times a dress or coat was made over from a garment given by a relative. One time she got a hand-me-down coat from Fru Christiansen. It had pretty, silver-colored buttons.

Money was scarce in those days following the great war. The first two years, 1914-1916, had been "boom" years for the Danish economy. Then came the unrestricted submarine campaign of the Kaiser's navy. The Danish government protested to no avail. The American entry into the war didn't bring any relief to the shortage of money in Denmark because the Allies enforced the rule: "No trade with the enemy." The British navy was everywhere on the seas. While rationing became a fact of life in Norway and Sweden, the Danes had enough to eat. Wages increased, too, but inflation went up two hundred percent during those four years of war.

The Russian Revolution brought anti-capitalist demonstrations. Those feelings were vented on the elections of 1918. The failure of the Danes to win back North Slesvig as a Danish territory brought a lowering of morale to Danish pride. Somehow, the Dannebrog did not glisten in the sunlight as it had in earlier days. This flag had been given from heaven as an assurance that Denmark, Europe's oldest monarchy, would last forever. Betty had learned this in school.

Fortunately, little boys and girls measure life's values by other standards than economic or political fortunes. Betty's childhood had been happy. Now in the early morning thunder storm moving through the Bronx and across Long Island, Betty felt herself in Denmark again. The Christmas carol written by Bishop Grundtvig, *"Deilig er den Himmel bla,"* touched her inner feelings. It boded well for her future. Maybe she and Erik would be married by Christmas! Not even the clouds of war and the enemy occupation could dullen her vision of *"Bright and glorious is the sky."*

If only Herr Christiansen could be there with his family. She remembered so well how, at age thirteen, he had given her a summer job at his house when school was out. She took care of the children, did the dishes, worked in the garden and ran errands. She even got to ask him questions about America, even though he himself had never been there. She was rewarded for her work with twenty-five kroner for the summer, about four dollars in American money, but it was all hers. When Betty was confirmed, she was old enough to get a job in town.

Now she slept soundly again. The sky outside was "bright and glorious" with an electrical storm. Betty heard nothing except Herr Christiansen singing her favorite carol. At the airport, mechanics were checking the engines and controls on the giant Clipper plane that would lift off over the Atlantic at noon. The weather report was for clear skies.

CHAPTER 8

Grandpa Christian

WO ROYAL FAMILIES have been the monarchs of Denmark since 1448. They both came from German background, the House of Oldenburg (1448-1863) and the House of Glucksburg (1863 to the present). With the one exception of King Hans (a shortening of Johannes or John) who ruled from 1481 to 1513, all the kings have been named either Christian or Frederick. There have been ten Christians and nine Fredericks. Margaret II became queen of Denmark in 1972. The only other woman to have such a distinction was Margrethe I who was queen from 1387-1397. She was a shrewd politician and in reality ruled from 1375 to 1412.

It's not surprising that so many families named their sons after royalty. Betty's grandfather was named Christian and he named one of his sons Martinus Christian, after Martin Luther and Christian IX, who was king during that son's birth. Norwegian and Swedish families did the same thing. They named their sons Karl (Carl in America), named after Karl XV who reigned from 1859-72; and Oscar, named after Oscar II, who reigned from 1872 to 1905 in Norway and until 1907 in Sweden, during the height of the immigration period. The Swedes also used Gustav and the Norwegians named sons Olaf and Haakon. People don't do that any more. The emigration period from Scandinavia is past and many people aren't that excited about royalty any more.

Betty was very fond her grandfather, Christian Kirkegaard (1859-1930). In later years she reflected that his name "Christian" well suited him. She saw the look of kindness in his face. A picture of Grandpa Christian and Grandma Marie taken in their later years revealed a kindly look on both of their faces. He wore a heavy mustache and a goatee which gave the appearance of distinction. Whoever saw him offered him respect.

Even at age sixty, grandpa Christian was strong and vigorous. On his last visit to America, when he was past sixty, he'd taken farm jobs near Albert Lea, Minnesota, while visiting his family who had immigrated to America. Work was not hard for his sturdy frame and long muscular arms. At the end of the work day, the young farm workers liked to show off their muscles in wrestling matches.

Grandpa Christian was not one to sit around and watch while others did things. He challenged the young bucks at their own game. At first, no one believed he was really serious. Finally, one burly young German farm boy thought he would show the other fellows he had the nerve. He had not counted on such a match. Grandpa Christian moved quick as a cat. In no time, the young challenger was flat on his back. There were a few more challenges, but not many. Grandpa Christian was king of the mat.

Back in Denmark, even when he was seventy, he'd walk to the North Sea beach by Tverstad, about six kilometers from

Bindslev. He'd shed his clothes and run into the ocean waves of the Skagerrak. Then he'd walk home again.

Twice married, Grandpa Christian took faithfully the church's admonition to rear his children "in the fear and the admonition of the Lord." When his first wife died, he advertised in a newspaper for a "Christian wife." Betty's mother was born of the second family. There was tender love, too, but no card playing, dancing, or liquor. While his children may not have always observed all of these prohibitions, they did keep his admonition to "love the Lord."

The name "Kirkegaard" literally means "church farm." It usually meant the farm next to the church. It can also mean "cemetery." The farmer who took care of the land and livestock sometimes was called "Kirkegaard." Grandpa Christian's father was the first of that family to baptize his children with the name Kirkegaard. The family had originally come from Vemb on the west coast of Jutland, not far from another family of the same name. The father of Soren Kierkegaard (1813-1855), the "father of modern existentialism," moved to Copenhagen from that region. There is, however, no known relationship. At an old age, Grandpa Christian's father pushed a cart and walked all the way to Bindslev to live on his son's farm for the rest of his life.

When Grandpa Christian died at age 72 on April 13, 1930, Grandma and Betty were left alone. It wasn't easy. They cried a lot. But Grandma comforted Betty, saying, "now he is with Jesus." Even many years later, Betty said: "I remember very plainly seeing Grandpa lying in the casket. He retained his look of dignity even in death. He even appeared to have the look of love on his face. I felt that he loved me very much. I could always feel it."

The funeral was held in the old church west of the village which still stands and is in use. It had been built in the 1100s and was white in color, both inside and out. On the inside, whitewash was put on to cover up the pictures of the "saints" painted before the Reformation. King Christian III made a law establishing "Lutheranism" to be the religion of the land in August 1536. Fifteen years earlier he had been with Martin Luther at Worms in southwest Germany. He heard the professor from Wittenberg say: "Hier stehe ich. Ich kan nicht anders. Gott helfe mir" ("Here I stand. I can do no other. God help me").

Grandpa Christian was buried in a plot close to the church entrance. It's alongside the walk used every Sunday. Danish cemeteries are kept immaculately clean and neat, with trees and flowers everywhere. Every Sunday when Betty goes to worship, she likes to linger in the cemetery before his gravestone. She still remembers Grandpa Christian with great fondness. His tombstone bears an inscription from II Timothy 4:7, "I have finished the race, I have kept the faith."

Leaving Home

CONFIRMATION WAS A SIGNIFICANT RITE of passage to young people growing up in Denmark. This ceremony of the church was the dividing line between being a child and an adult. It meant a new suit for boys and a new white dress for girls. It also meant being admitted to the sacrament of Holy Communion.

Confirmation was held when a boy or girl was ready to leave home and go to work. In rural Jutland that was usually on a neighboring farm. The money earned was often paid to the parents to help support the family at home. It was a definite break with the past and usually took place when a child was between thirteen and fifteen years old. Going on to higher education was not for every youth. It was reserved for a privileged few. The money earned was badly needed by the family.

Betty worked at many jobs before she went to America. Because it was hard to earn enough money to take care of her needs, Betty did what many other young people in Denmark did when they wanted to better themselves. She went to Copenhagen to look for work. She especially liked to take care of children; in fact, she'd only take jobs in homes where there were children. But she also worked in bakeries and restaurants. Anyone who has visited an authentic Danish bakery knows that this is where some of the best smells in the world can be found.

Betty felt fortunate to find a position in a home with children. She was happy there. One night while she was putting the children to bed, an express letter arrived from Bindslev. The contents froze her heart: "Dear Betty, I have sad news for you. Your Grandma Marie died." Grandma Marie had been a strong emotional and spiritual support to Betty. She cried all through the night, thinking over and over: "Dear Grandma, I miss you so much. Now I have no mother in Denmark." In between her tears, she started to sing a hymn, "Let us decide to meet in heaven."

The next morning there was nothing to do but give up her job and go to the train station to buy a ticket for Bindslev. Copenhagen is on the island of Zealand, which the Danes call Sjaelland (pronounced SHAY-lund). That meant the train had to pass over the "Great Belt" a body of water between Sjaelland and Jutland. Jutland is a peninsula attached to Germany on the south. The journey could easily be made in a day. Everything went well on the trip and Betty was met at the train station by her relatives.

The funeral was held in the church at the edge of town and Grandma Marie was buried alongside Grandpa Christian. During the service, Betty tried hard to listen to the sermon and participate in the liturgy. But she was gripped by a feeling of lonesomeness. "What will I do now?" she thought.

After the service, her aunt Magdalena, her mother's youngest sister, came up to Betty and said: "Betty, why don't you come and stay with me a while?" Betty thought well of the idea as she didn't have a home in Bindslev anymore. Besides, there would be children in the home. It would help Betty to overcome her lonesomeness. She stayed for almost half a year. Realizing that her aunt's home belonged to her cousins and not to her, she decided that she had to return to Copenhagen again.

Betty found her first employment at the YWCA serving meals. It was a job which helped pay bills, but it didn't satisfy her for long. She took another job and that wasn't the right one either. Finally she found one she liked, working in a home for a woman who was a music teacher and whose husband worked at the library. They treated her with warm hospitality and kindness and tried hard to become a family for Betty. Her spirits were lifted and she came to dearly love the two little boys in the home. They helped to take away the pain of Grandma Marie's death.

Little noticed by Betty and most Danes, ominous things were happening in Denmark's neighbor to the south. The Versailles Treaty forced on Germany after the Great War had reduced the nation to extreme poverty. There were Communist demonstrations and the long arm of the Soviet Union's subversive activities started to alarm the people. The economy failed. It was said by some that it took a wheelbarrow full of German marks to buy a loaf of bread. That may be an exaggeration, but the nation had become desperate and they elected Adolf Hitler to be Chancellor in March of 1933. He promised better times and appealed to German nationalism. He wasted no time in taking complete control of the government. He promised prosperity and security to the people and set the wheels of industry rolling again. The Weimar government established after the war was not able to stand against Hitler's aggressive march to power. Hitler appeared to many people to be just what the country needed. He had admirers all over the western world.

The people of Denmark, of course, could not help noticing the changes taking place on their southern border. Many were amazed at the happenings and were pleased that poverty was being relieved. Still, there were some who kept a wary eye on their giant neighbor and were distrustful of its new leadership.

But Denmark should have nothing to fear. Germany had suffered a disastrous defeat in the war and she was forbidden to rearm. So everything must be all right. Why should they worry?

The international scene was not Betty's concern. She was learning to live by herself without Grandma Marie's guidance. She was actually becoming happy again.

"Wonderful Copenhagen"

COPENHAGEN IS AN OLD CITY founded by Bishop Absalon in the twelfth century. The name means a "market harbor," it was an early place of commerce.

Copenhagen can be an exciting place, especially for a country girl raised on a farm in the northern tip of Jutland. There was an endless variety of things to do and to see. There was also a difference in the mood of people living in Denmark's largest city and the rural folk. Copenhagen offered all kinds of entertainment and merriment, whereas the rural folks lived a simpler life and thought more about the virtues of hard work.

Anyone who has been to Copenhagen has seen Tivoli, one of the most entertaining places in Europe. All summer long there are concerts, stage plays including mime shows, a wax museum with life-like facsimiles of famous persons, wonderful eating places, and rides that will rival any state fair. Just outside the entrance to Tivoli is a large statue of Hans Christian Andersen sitting with a book, reading fairy tales. It's also a place to relax, meet friends and to let the mind wander. In Copenhagen there are castles to visit, large churches, museums, canal rides, and shops with the most interesting things on the shelves. It's everything a girl from the country could want. It could be a never-ending place to have a good time.

Betty never felt alone in Copenhagen. She had an abundance of good friends, many of them like her, having come from farms throughout Denmark. But Betty remembered the teaching of her Grandmother and of the parish pastor who taught her confirmation class. She was serious about her Christian faith. By the time Betty was fifteen she knew that her life was in the hands of the Lord and she wanted to serve him.

During that time in Copenhagen, Betty encountered the Oxford Movement. It gave renewal to her spiritual life. This movement originated in the Nineteenth Century at Oxford University in England. The leaders wanted to return to the teachings of the early and undivided church. They desired a deeper spirituality and encouraged a renewal of private confession. One of the lasting influences of the Oxford Movement is found in the practice of mutual confession in Alcoholics Anonymous. One of its founders had been influenced by the movement. Betty found the Oxford Movement to be challenging and helpful in shaping her early adult life. She needed such a group contact because fear would sometimes come over her. Not even all the fun things of Copenhagen could protect her from it.

For all the dangerous things that can happen to a young woman in a large city, Betty lived a very sheltered life. She wasn't the adventurous kind who took unnecessary chances about her personal safety, nor was she attracted to the wild parties for which she had abundant opportunities. Hers was a simple faith, and she looked every day for the guidance of God in her life.

The lure of the big city with all its glamour did not fulfill Betty's feeling for life. Even though she had many good friends, and a wonderful home in which to live with the music teacher. Something else was beckoning: Her real mother. Was this the time to go to America? Was the New World to be her destiny as it had become for so many of the Kirkegaard family? Would she now be welcomed or would she be in the way? She would wait and test her inner urges.

America was always big news in Denmark because so many Danes had immigrated there. Not far from her home, the largest American Independence Day celebration outside of the USA was held every July 4th. In the heather-clad hills of Rebild, fifteen miles south of Arhus in north Jutland, enthusiastic crowds gathered every year. At the first celebration in 1912, ten thousand people attended, headed by King Christian X and Queen Alexandrine, despite a pouring rain. The celebration at Rebild was a bonding with more than 1,500,000 Americans who claimed Danish roots. Abraham Lincoln had long been a great hero to the Scandinavian people. In 1934, a log cabin museum was built in his honor with logs from every state in the USA in which Danes lived.

The goal of the leaders who organized the event was to perpetuate strong ties of friendship between the two countries and to instill a feeling of love for Denmark among younger Danish-Americans. The influence of this celebration and its excitement was not lost on Betty's family, especially since many had left Denmark for this land of opportunity.

But America was in the midst of the Great Depression. Money was scarce. Drought and huge dust storms had covered the Great Plains. Wages were low and good jobs were almost impossible to find. Besides that, Betty didn't have the special skills that American industry needed. In fact, her education had stopped short of high school. In 1936, Franklin Roosevelt had just been elected president for a second term. Strikes were paralyzing many industries in the land. Communism, Fascism, and anarchy were raising a scare.

The Danish newspapers reported that the American government had ordered six million pigs killed during September 1934 because of a feed shortage caused by the drought. Many people in Denmark talked about this as the pork industry was at the backbone of the Danish economy. The Danes had started the first pork cooperative in the world. Was America really on the right track? Many questioned if this was a good time to leave Denmark for America. Betty would have to make up her own mind.

Decision America

TRAVEL BETWEEN EUROPE AND AMERICA is a simple matter today. Even students jaunt between the two continents as easily as if they were going home for the holidays. That was not the case in 1937. Travel for ordinary people was by ocean liner. Only the rich could afford to ride the new Pan Am Clipper planes.

Betty agonized and was torn between the desire to see her birth mother and the expense of the trip. Once Betty left her grandparents' home in Bindslev, she realized that this would never be her home again. When she returned from Copenhagen for her Grandmother's funeral, the old house was sold. She no longer had a home in Bindslev. And as much as she enjoyed Copenhagen and the family which had opened their home to her, she knew in her heart that this was not to be a permanent home.

A girl in Denmark in those days couldn't just say, "I'm going to America." There were a lot of things to consider. Where would she get the money for the trip? It might take Betty years to save up that much money in Denmark. There was another thing that bothered people travelling to the Midwest United States. They would have to go through Chicago.

Chicago had a reputation for crime and violence. Perhaps the best known American in Europe was Al Capone. Would Betty be risking her life to make such a trip? The St. Valentine's Day Massacre of 1929 had become news around the world. Capone's gang, dressed as policemen, had murdered another rival gang in cold blood. How could one tell the difference between real policemen and gangsters dressed as policemen? It would be well to think twice before going through Chicago.

Whenever Betty had a problem that stood as a brick wall in front of her, she would pray. And then she'd leave it in the hands of God. She would be content to accept whatever happened.

On one of his trips to Denmark, Betty's Uncle Chris from Albert Lea, Minnesota, heard about Betty's wish to go to America to see her mother. Uncle Chris got word to her saying, "I'll loan you money so you can go to your mother." Her uncle was the son of Grandpa Christian's first wife. The Kirkegaards, however, were a closely knit family. Uncle Chris didn't hesitate to offer his assistance, but since he was also a businessman, it would be a loan. He had come to America with nothing more than an ambition to get ahead. He developed a tiling business and was responsible for draining many fields in southern Minnesota.

All the roadblocks seemed to have now disappeared. Why should she not go to America? Betty approached everything with caution. She would have to plan the trip with care. There would be a steamship ticket to buy. Which liner should she choose? Would there be anyone she would know on board the ship? Betty was not unused to being alone in Denmark, but she wanted to find some people to be her friends on the long ocean voyage. She'd feel so much safer if there were another family or person with whom she could visit and confide as they crossed the ocean. Betty prayed again. She had always trusted that God would provide.

Since her grandmother died, events in Europe were moving swiftly. What some people feared, appeared to be happening. Not only had Hitler marched into the Rhine valley to occupy land held by Germany before the war, but he was making threatening sounds all around his borders where ethnic Germans were living. His aim was to reincorporate them back into Germany and then, many suspected, to take over the neighboring lands as well. If Betty were thinking mainly of herself, going to America might seem the best thing to do. But what about her uncles, aunts and cousins in Denmark? But then, that was really an unfounded fear.

Germany had not threatened Denmark since the Slesvig-Holstein War of 1864. Denmark had acted unwisely in annexing the province of Slesvig into its own nation, separating it from Holstein. Because there were many Germans living there, it gave Otto von Bismarck, the new and little known Prime minister of Prussia, the excuse to try out his new army. He needed to win prestige. Even though the Danes withdrew, Bismarck ordered the combined Austrian and Prussian army of sixty thousand with modern equipment to advance against the Danish force of forty thousand with old equipment. The Danes were severely routed. They had trusted in the Danevirke, an earthen embankment which was a thousand years old, for their defense. Such historical romanticism did not match Bismarck's realism about war.

That had been over seventy years ago and their borders had been at peace since. It's true that in 1920, after the Great War, a vote was held in Slesvig giving the people a chance to decide whether they wanted to belong to Denmark or Germany. So many Germans had moved to Slesvig that the province was divided. The north part went to Denmark and the south remained in Germany. The Danes in Slesvig were eager to be returned to Danish rule. Five thousand Danes from North Slesvig had lost their lives fighting for the Kaiser's army. After the plebiscite, King Christian X rode across the frontier on horseback and North Slesvig was reunited with Denmark.

Small nations need good memories, especially if they border powerful nations with a history of military conflict. The Danes remembered and Betty had learned these lessons well in school. So, as in the Great War of 1914-1918, they bent every effort to be a neutral nation. They just wanted the freedom to trade.

It was settled. Betty would go to America. Her family on both sides of the ocean was excited for her.

Homecoming To Mother

BETTY HAD HEARD that she had a mother in America. She was only four when her mother left Denmark for America. Her mother worked part time and when she went to America, her memory vanished from Betty's mind. During all these years Betty had lived with her grandparents and thought of her grandmother as her mother.

Leaving Betty behind in Denmark wasn't easy for her mother. But John, the one to whom she was promised, wanted her to come to America and to marry her. Finally she went, greatly distressed to leave Betty behind. Her emotional anxiety became so serious that some wondered if she would lose her mind completely. It was agreed that someone would bring Betty to her mother, but it never happened. Betty's mother had three children in America. They needed her attention and this distracted her from thinking constantly about Betty.

Betty was twelve years old before Grandma Marie told her one day, "Betty, I think maybe you should go to live with your mother in America." It would be eleven years until that reunion could take place. But finally Betty's arrangements were complete. The ticket was purchased to cross the Atlantic on a

Swedish boat. The best part was that she had met a family from Sweden visiting in Denmark who were crossing the ocean on the same voyage. Betty felt her prayers being answered. She would not be alone on the trip.

The ship left Copenhagen in June 1937. It was a good thing the Swedish family was looking after her, because Betty became terribly seasick once they started plowing through the big ocean waves. It's quite a jolt to both body and mind when the ship starts to weave sideways and to lurch forward. Would the ship hold together or was this first ocean voyage also her last? It would take over a week to make the crossing.

Fortunately, like most people, Betty got over her seasickness in time to enjoy a part of the voyage. And of course, one just had to feel good when the captain's dinner was held. This was the high point of the trip. Everybody got dressed up in their best clothes for the formal affair. It was a night to remember.

When the ocean liner at last arrived in New York, they sailed past the Statue of Liberty welcoming them to America. Now the scary business started all over again. Who would meet her? Would they be there? What if they weren't? How would she ever get to Racine to find her mother?

It was an exciting moment when Betty said goodbye to her Swedish friends and stood on solid ground again. And there they were, Uncle Martin and Aunt Esther. They had come from Albany to meet her. It was a moment of tears and joy. She had finally arrived in America and she wasn't alone. Betty didn't think of this just as a coincidence. Someone was watching over her. Her prayers were being answered.

Uncle Martin couldn't just go straight home to Albany. This called for some excitement. The Kirkegaards were always fun-loving people. Betty had to see some of the sights, so they sailed up the Hudson River. During the night she saw the bright lights all along the shore. It was a glorious homecoming to America.

Then Betty saw something she had not seen before: Black servants. Black people were not strangers to Denmark for Denmark had once owned the Danish West Indies (now called Virgin Islands), where blacks make up about 80% of the population. Denmark sold the islands to the United States in 1916. So there were black people who spoke fluent Danish. But she had never seen them as a class of servants before. In Denmark they were just like the Danes, except, of course, for the color of their skin. She would soon have more surprises.

Betty stayed two eventful weeks in Albany. Then it was time to move on to meet her mother. For the train ride to Chicago she was all alone. Again she wondered, would her mother be there to meet her? Would they find each other in the big crowds at the railway station? Would they recognize each other?

Betty's mother and her husband, John, were waiting for Betty when the train arrived. They recognized each other instantly. Betty's mother looked enough like her sisters in Denmark, so identification was not difficult. However, Betty's mother was surprised to see her daughter now as a handsome young woman, not the little girl she had left behind. "My, how tall you have grown," she said. Also greeting Betty at the train station was Mrs. Schneller, whom she would come to know and appreciate as a helpful friend. Mrs. Schneller's husband was a medical doctor in Racine.

They drove by automobile from Union Station near the heart of Chicago's Loop, an area which was encircled by the elevated train tracks, and which enclosed much of the city's important businesses. The buildings were so tall. They didn't have such skyscrapers in Denmark, not even in Copenhagen.

They finally made it through the city traffic and got on the highway going north to Racine. Here they went through a number of small cities and past many beautiful fields of corn and other grains. The fields were so big compared to the neat little farms of Denmark. But this was America. Everything had to be bigger here.

They finally arrived in Racine and drove up to the house on Wright Avenue. This was the home of John and Cecelia Poulson and their three children, Roy, Maynard and Delores – Betty's family in America. Her new life was about to begin.

CHAPTER 13

Learning To Live In America

*D*R. SCHNELLER was a physician in a general practice. His wife, Hazel, became Betty's tutor in America. They had taken a liking to the Poulsons, Betty's family. The Poulsons lived on the second floor of the Schneller home. It was of mutual benefit. Papa John, as Betty called him, was handy in doing things about the place, such as putting on the storm windows.

The first thing Mrs. Schneller said to Betty after they had gotten settled was, "To live in America you must learn to speak English." At that time English was not taught in the Danish schools as it is today. Danish children are now required to learn English and they are taught to speak it with a British accent. Before leaving Denmark, Betty had taken some English lessons in evening classes, so it wasn't altogether a strange sounding tongue. When the Schnellers moved into a new house, Betty's family continued to rent the second floor apartment in their old house. Betty, however, moved with the Schnellers and worked for them.

Every morning Mrs. Schneller and Betty would read English. Dr. Schneller prodded her to learn English too. One of

Betty's jobs at the Schneller home was to answer the telephone. When she spoke Danish on the phone, the doctor would say, "Betty, we don't allow anyone to swear in this house." Her language skills were improving, but Betty wanted to speak English so she would sound like a native-born American. So, she enrolled in a correspondence course with the University of Wisconsin. Mrs. Schneller continued to be her tutor.

Betty did so well in her exams that she was able to go to high school, even though she was much older than the other students. She attended high school for two years. She really thought that she ought to graduate, but by that time she was twenty-four years old. She needed to get out on her own.

These were happy years, being reunited with her mother and getting to know her two brothers and younger sister. Having a younger sister provided Betty with a deep joy like she had never known before. They became very close. Betty admits to probably spoiling her, but it was so much fun. By this time Betty felt that America would be home for the rest of her life. She had become comfortable in the New World and was starting to forget Denmark. She liked living in Racine by Lake Michigan. She especially liked to attend church and found a lot of friends in the church youth group.

There comes a time, however, when young people need to move out of their parental homes and make a life for themselves. So, Betty started to move towards Chicago. First she found work in Highland Park and later in Winnetka. Again she found a church with young people. She felt safe with them. However, she hadn't forgotten her instincts of self-preservation. Once when a man whom she had never seen before wanted her to go with him to his car, she thought better of it. Even in church, a stranger may pose danger.

Betty remembered what her grandmother once told her when, as a teen-ager, a boy-friend broke up with her: "Betty, God has something very good in store for you." She never forgot those words. They stuck to her and guided her steps many times.

In the meantime, Betty and Erik began corresponding. It was just a friendly exchange of letters with someone she had known back in Denmark. They had known each other as small children and had played together. So it was comforting to share thoughts across the ocean with someone from her past.

One day, however, a different kind of letter arrived from Erik in Denmark. He asked her to marry him! Erik was musically talented and enclosed a song which he had written that expressed his desires, complete with piano notes. Betty was stunned. She had just taken it for granted that she'd always live in America like so many of her family. Now she had to make a decision. It would mean leaving her mother whom she had waited so long to see. They had become very close to each other. And Papa John, too, he had been so kind to her. Then there was her little sister. How could she ever leave them?

Betty's family was predictably upset with the prospect that she might return to Denmark. Of course, they'd miss her. But this was 1939 and the economy was improving in America. If Betty wanted to work, good jobs were becoming more numerous. She could marry someone in America. There were plenty of young Danish men in Racine who would make good husbands.

They assumed that Erik must be a fine man and worthy of Betty's hand and Denmark was still dear to their hearts. But there was one other thing to consider. Conditions in Europe were worsening.

Hitler and his gang of Nazis were behaving dangerously. Just the year before Germany had annexed Austria and imposed its iron rule on the people. Through bluff, threats, and lies, Hitler persuaded the British Prime Minister, Neville Chamberlain, to agree to a division of Czechoslovakia, ceding a large area where Germans lived, to Germany. The British were told, "there will be peace in our time." Shortly after this happened, Poland grabbed a slice of Czechoslovakia to add to its southern border. Things didn't sound good.

The Danes were nervous, too, and so they agreed to sign a nonaggression pact with Germany in May 1939, hoping that this would guarantee their neutrality. Hitler claimed that he would be satisfied with the territorial gains he had made bringing the Germans back into Germany. Each time Hitler made a new land grab, however, his general staff was opposed to the move. But when the western powers kept pacifying Hitler, their hands were tied, and he became bolder.

Betty pondered all these things. So she did what she always did when making decisions. She prayed and waited for God's answer. Erik, her childhood playmate's image grew larger in her mind every day. Love had been awakened in her heart and made the decision for her. She would go back to Denmark. It sounded dangerous to her family and friends, maybe even crazy. Denmark was beckoning her heart to return.

CHAPTER 14

Erik

ERIK WAITED ANXIOUSLY for Betty's answer to his marriage proposal. He was overjoyed when word finally came that Betty would be his bride.

The name "Waehrens" has a German background. Erik did not know the history of how the name got into Denmark. It was, however, the custom of Danish kings to appoint Germans of the lower nobility to positions of responsibility in government and commerce. That was a way to strengthen their authority. The kings of Denmark had their roots in German royalty since 1448. Since Denmark and Norway were ruled by the same monarchs from 1380 to 1814, many Germans were also appointed to high positions in Norway and then became Norwegian.

Erik grew up in Bindslev, the third oldest of ten children. He had five brothers and four sisters. His father, John Waehrens, had a large tailor shop. He also manufactured clothes for both men and women. Erik was the only one who learned the tailor trade. In later years he took over the tailoring while his older brother, Kaj, managed the men's clothing department. Another brother, Paul, was also involved in the family business.

It may seem strange that Erik should all of a sudden start writing to Betty in America after all these years. It had begun when they were little children. They used to jump rope together. It was a game in which a person jumped on a certain letter of the alphabet. Then that was the initial of the person you were going to marry. Erik always jumped at the sound of the letter "B." Betty would jump at the letter "E." Betty had thought no more about it, but Erik kept the remembrance of the game in his heart. He knew then that he wanted to marry Betty someday, but, of course, didn't tell anyone about his secret.

After Betty had been in America for two years, Erik realized that if he wanted to have his childhood dream come true, he'd better do something about it. Of course, he didn't just write a letter saying, "Will you marry me?" He went through an intermediary, another girl, who gave the letters to Betty. It was some time before Erik dared to propose marriage because he was afraid he'd be rejected. After all, Betty was in America, thousands of miles away, and there were many young men who'd liked to have married Betty. But she had no serious boyfriends in America, though she could have. The problem was that the ones she really liked were already engaged.

One reason that Betty thought seriously about marrying Erik was that she had known him since childhood. She felt safer with him. She was afraid of marrying a stranger. Perhaps he would hide something important from her. She trusted Erik. Even when they were small children, an aunt would take care of Erik and bring him along home to her grandmother's house. She didn't know it then, but Erik already liked Betty at that tender age.

Not long after Erik's marriage proposal to Betty, war broke out in Europe. Germany invaded Poland. England and France declared war on Germany. For a while it looked like there would be no war on the western front. Neither side made any move. But Erik was worried. What if full scale fighting broke out? Would Betty still agree to marry him? Would it be safe for her to even try to return to Denmark?

While Betty and Erik were both saving up money for her return to Denmark, the most crushing blow fell. Despite their non-aggression pact of 1939, the German war machine stormed into Denmark early on the morning of April 9, 1940. For both Betty and Erik it looked like the end of their dream. Denmark's borders were sealed. All mail going out and coming into Denmark was censored by the Germans. What had Denmark done to offend Hitler? What did he want with that small country anyway?

All through the winter of 1939-40, Vidkun Quisling had made trips to Germany urging Hitler to occupy Norway. At first, Hitler didn't seem interested. He had his eyes set on conquering the Lowlands and France. Denmark posed no threat to his ambitions. But Quisling persisted and found support with some of the German military leaders. He finally persuaded Hitler that if he didn't occupy Norway, the English would. This would cut off Germany's supply of steel from Sweden, which was shipped from Narvik in the north of Norway and carried along the west coast to Germany. In fact, the English were thinking about that very thing. The problem was that Germany got there first.

But why Denmark? Hitler needed Denmark for the Luftwaffe, the German Air Force, to be in control over the skies of southern Norway. He also wanted to fortify the coastlands of Denmark so that the English could not invade the continent. Wars were being fought on a larger scale than ever before. One month after organized resistance ceased in Norway, Hitler launched his blitzkrieg, lightning war, against Holland, Belgium, and into France itself. Before the summer had hardly begun, western Europe was becoming a Nazi fortress.

Now things became complicated. Would Betty be able to obtain the visas necessary for travelling? And there was still the problem of money. Erik had promised to send her five hundred dollars and she hoped to save two hundred. But how would Erik manage to send the money? Would it be enough? Her life would have been so much simpler if Erik's marriage proposal had failed to arrive. But that was not her wish. She wanted to return with all her heart. She was committed. If the Lord would provide the way, she would go.

Erik's and Betty's dreams appeared to have fallen victim to the demonic powers of war. Were their hopes ever to be? Would Betty, in the safety of America, have her heart crushed again? It didn't look good. Once more, Betty prayed; and once more, she received the assurance, "Don't be afraid. Return to Denmark."

When The War Came To Denmark

PRIL 9, 1940, was Denmark's "Day of Infamy." Erik woke up that morning at six o'clock to a thundering noise. His little sister, Ruth, came running to his room, shouting, "Erik, get up!" They went outside to the steps. It was a beautiful spring morning. Together with many other people of the town, they looked up at the blue sky where hundreds of large, black airplanes flew very low over the town, heading northwards. They were German transports carrying troops for the invasion of Norway. Erik and his friends stood brokenhearted. "Poor Norway," were their first thoughts.

Men clenched their fists and cried in the streets when they heard over the radio that Denmark had been occupied by the Germans. That same day, German soldiers came on motorcycles and cars, all of them with a black kerchief over their faces. "We were occupied. I can't describe our feelings," Erik said later. He was twenty-four years old at the time.

It was especially troubling for Erik that morning. He had been with the Danish Navy in London in 1937 for the crowning of King George VI. There had been English, French, German, and Japanese military personnel, all professing friendship. Didn't the exchange of friendship between nations mean anything? Gone now were those exciting days when the seas were safe and honor was held sacred between people of many lands.

Unknown to Erik, the invasion had begun a few minutes before five o'clock that morning. The invasion of Denmark and Norway was called "Weseruebung." There had been plenty warning. Just the day before on April 8, large numbers of German warships were passing through the Danish straits. Alarmed, the Danish Prime Minister of Foreign Affairs went to see the German Minister and was assured that nothing was planned against Denmark. The very next morning, just before dawn, the same German Minister awakened the Prime Minister with an ultimatum which amounted to surrender. The Danes were given one hour to comply – or else!

The Prime Minister saw the German bombers darkening the sky and was informed that large German forces had landed on the islands and were crossing the border of South Jutland. It was impossible in that short time to assemble the members of the Cabinet to meet with the King. Before the hour was up, there was fighting in the streets.

Denmark could only muster about six thousand men effectively under arms. Ten times that amount were arrayed against them. The King and Cabinet agreed to the terms of the ultimatum, but "under protest." At noon the Government issued a proclamation. The King urged the people to be levelheaded and dignified in their behavior. The Germans agreed not to interfere in Denmark's internal affairs, and to respect Danish integrity and independence. This promise did not last the first day. Gestapo agents came by the thousands and Nazi propaganda was everywhere. Then they looted the national treasury to pay for the occupation.

In Copenhagen, invasion combat forces silently disembarked from the troopship "Hansestadt Danzig." They swarmed into the Citadel, the central military headquarters. The German soldiers had been hidden in a vessel which was supposed to contain coal to be delivered to Denmark. Little did the unsuspecting Danes realize that high German military officials had actually been in Copenhagen that very week to scout the city to determine Danish readiness. They were nervous about the attack. They needn't have been. At the same time Jutland and the island of Fyn were also occupied with only token resistance. Pro-Nazi Danish citizens wearing swastikas were directing traffic for the Germans and were shouting "Heil Hitler."

The Germans dropped leaflets from the sky telling the people that Denmark was under German protection and that resistance was useless. Many mysteries surfaced. Why had the chief of the navy given all the men of the coast batteries the day off on April 8? Why were the ships that carried German soldiers to Denmark owned by a Danish businessman? He had been known to have had some shady transactions in the last war. Was justice done when he died suddenly, soon afterwards, in Germany?

King Christian X had openly scorned the warning that his country was in danger. On the evening of April 8th, the king was advised that Denmark might be invaded. He replied that he couldn't "really believe that" and went off to the theatre to watch a performance of the "Merry Wives of Windsor." Perhaps he placed too much confidence in the anti-aggression pact signed at Germany's request in May 1939. Or perhaps he knew that the invasion was inevitable and decided that he would save his country from the kind of destruction experienced by the Poles.

Why had the invasion succeeded so brilliantly? Totalitarian governments always have the initial advantage in war. They are not bothered with a free press or the need for parliamentary debates. Neither do they have to explain and justify their actions to their people.

A short time before this, Winston Churchill had announced that England could not accept responsibility for the defense of Denmark in case it was attacked. A member of the English parliament had said just a year before at a private dinner in Copenhagen, "While nobody expects you to resist physically, we expect you to give the best example of passive resistance the world has seen." That the Danes did magnificently. One distinguished Dane said: "Ours is not a glamorous position. We can't compete when it comes to being executed; perhaps not even in being looted."

In Washington, the Danish Ambassador Kauffmann, severed all ties with the government in Copenhagen. He declared himself a representative of "Free Denmark." He made a treaty which placed Greenland under American protection. The Danish merchant marine refused to obey the German command to return to Denmark. They entered the war on the side of Hitler's enemies.

This was a dark day for Erik. How would Betty be able to return to Denmark now?

CHAPTER 16

Betty Reconsiders

*H*ITLER WAS SUPREMELY CONFIDENT as 1940 ended. True, he had not forced England to surrender, but that would be only a matter of time. They would not be able to withstand the continual punishment from the air that the Luftwaffe rained on them. In fact, he boasted to Mussolini as they met at the Brenner Pass on October 4: "The war is won!"

Hundreds of children left London to escape the night raids. By the middle of October, almost a half a million children had been evacuated. President Roosevelt helped keep hope alive for the English when he declared: "We will continue to help those who resist aggression, and who now hold the aggressors far from our shores." The English talked a brave line, but Hitler screamed: "Let's wait and see what London looks like two or three months from now."

In America, Betty's family listened attentively to the radio reports on the war. Most of the news was on the plight of Britain, but they kept straining their ears to find out what might be happening in Denmark. News commentators were eagerly listened to by the whole nation. H. V. Kaltvenborn in his stentorian tones; Gabriel Heater with his staccato speech; and Dorothy Thompson with her biased accusations against her enemy list, greatly influenced how Americans felt, even though the United States was technically neutral.

Betty's mother and family tried their best to change her mind about returning to Denmark. The evidence was all on their side. She would be placing herself in needless danger to live under the Nazi rule. Besides that, they would probably lose contact with her, especially if America and Germany became combatants.

Betty's mind wavered. You couldn't blame her if she reconsidered her decision to return to Denmark. Some people went so far as to tell Betty: "You're crazy to even think about it!" Some argued that perhaps Erik could get permission to come to America or maybe the war would soon be over and then things would be better. Betty felt all alone in this struggle. Everyone thought she should change her mind about marrying Erik now.

The war was widening. Italy entered the war on the Nazi side. The war had also spread to North Africa. Yugoslavia and Greece were occupied by the Germans. Crete fell. Not much help could be expected from America to the threatened democracies. President Roosevelt promised the American people just a few days before the election of 1940: "Your boys are not going to be sent into any foreign wars."

Before Germany attacked the Soviet Union on June 22, 1941, the Communists in Denmark had been non-cooperative in any Danish Resistance work. They held to their own agenda, on orders from Moscow, and cooperated with the Germans. But within one week, June 29, they published the first edition of their underground newspaper, "Land and People." This did not mean that they were true allies to the other Danes. But every enemy of the Nazi regime was a sign of encouragement to the Danish people. And much as the Danes in America feared the Bolsheviks, they welcomed another front against Hitler. The problem was that the Germans were everywhere victorious on the Eastern front.

The Danes, despite their apparent helpless condition, were not passive. The Free Danish Movement was established in London June 26, 1940, and they appealed to all Danes in Great Britain to rally behind them. Some of them began secretly training for sabotage work in their homeland. They were dropped by parachute into Denmark to organize the Resistance. Broadcasts from England were directed to the Danish people. The opening notes from Beethoven's Fifth Symphony became their call to victory in opposing the enemy. Resistance in Denmark came under the command of the Special Operations Executive (SOE), a department of England's war strategy.

Because this was kept secret, Betty couldn't know what was being planned for making Denmark free again. Neither could Erik write what he might have heard about it to her. The Nazis had cruel ways of extracting information out of people whom they suspected of opposing their regime.

In the whirlwinds passing through Betty's mind, she almost forgot the most important thing about the trip. She would need money. Working at the Schnellers for board and room plus a small stipend didn't allow her to save much. How could she save the $200 she needed? And how could Erik get the $500 out of Denmark to send to her with the Nazis in such tight control? It really did look impossible. It was a case of a willing spirit, but weak flesh. How could a young man in Denmark and his fiancee, thousands of miles away in America, triumph over the mad man in Berlin?

If Betty was not going back to Denmark, Erik would have to know. The stress was just as hard on him as it was on her. What she couldn't really be sure of was what was really happening in Bindslev. Her uncles, aunts, and cousins were living under the occupation. She was willing to share their unhappy plight, if only she could get there.

The summer of 1941 moved slowly for Betty. What if the German armies should crush the Russian defenses before winter set in? They then would turn their victorious military forces against the western democracies and there would be no hope for Denmark or for her and Erik. Hitler's new order would threaten the whole world.

Betty put her decision into the hands of God. She prayed for assurance. It wasn't easy because it looked impossible. But hers was a simple faith. She finally decided that if God wanted her to go, the way would be provided. She'd rest her case. But in the face of her family's opposition, the decision was hers. No one could decide for her. She would do the will of God!

Betty Makes Her Plans

*B*ETTY NEEDED MONEY to buy a Clipper ticket to Denmark. She left the Schnellers in Racine to work for a wealthy family in Highland Park, north of Chicago. After five months, she realized that she wouldn't get to Denmark working for them. After all, people don't become wealthy by giving it away. Then she went to work for a lawyer. She started at eleven dollars a week and worked up to eighteen. At that time it seemed like loads of money, but not enough to pay for the Clipper fare.

About a year after leaving Racine, she got a letter from Erik. Enclosed was the five hundred dollars he had promised to send. It was difficult to get the money out of Denmark, but love can conquer many obstacles, including the Nazi Occupation.

This called for action. Betty immediately got new hope and started making plans for her return to Denmark. It involved many trips to Chicago. Travel was simplified by using the electric train which ran between Chicago and Milwaukee.

The British Embassy couldn't understand why Betty wanted to make the trip. They explained to her all the complications and dangers which she would have to face. "Miss Poulson," the clerk said, "I know that you want to return to Denmark to get married. But it is not advisable at this time. No one knows how long this war will last. The Nazis are often unpredictably treacherous in their treatment of people. We can probably issue the visa for travel, but we don't think anyone should go there now. You would have to travel through Berlin and it has been heavily bombed in recent weeks."

Betty was downhearted many times. It was tempting to send the money back and live out the war in America. She almost gave up many times. It seemed that the whole world was against her. But since Erik had sent the money he'd promised for the trip, how could she back out now? Again she found strength in Psalm 103, *"The Lord is merciful and gracious, slow to anger and abounding in steadfast love."* It was not just Betty's decision to return, she was sure it was the will of God. There could be no second thoughts. Since her decision was made, there was no time to lose. Conditions in Europe might change which would make it impossible to return.

There were so many things for Betty to do before she was ready to leave. One of them was to go shopping for a wedding dress. So one day Betty, her mother and little sister, went to Milwaukee to go shopping. She had saved up money for the purchase of the dress, veil and shoes. That was an exciting day in her life. It was already August and the Clipper flight from New York was scheduled for September 7. Things were falling into place. The obstacles in America were being solved. Except for one thing: Her family. They would try one more time to convince her to wait. They tried to no avail. Betty's face was set for Europe.

The family had good reasons. The Russian Front seemed to be on the verge of collapse. Hitler was jubilant. He was determined that there should not be "any military power West of the Urals, even if we have to fight a hundred years' war to prevent it." Reports were leaking out that the murder of Jews was a daily occurrence. On July 17, seven hundred Jews had been taken out of Vilna in Lithuania to a nearby holiday resort and had been shot. These statistics were being carefully compiled in Berlin. This was going on everywhere in Eastern Europe where Jews lived. Death squads also operated against Russians.

The British, it turned out, had obtained a secret decoding machine called the Enigma. It had been smuggled out of Poland. With it they were able to learn what German generals were reporting to Berlin about the execution of civilians. They also learned something else. The German progress against the Russians was not going so well as the German propaganda would like the world to believe. There were increasing casualties on the Eastern front. The Luftwaffe was no longer able to provide adequate air protection to their soldiers on the front or to strategic positions in the rear. Churchill ordered that information sent to Stalin.

Unknown to Betty and Erik, and to most of the world, the British spy system had learned that Germany was working on an atomic bomb. The British began working to develop their own bomb.

Meanwhile back in America, Betty's proposed trip to Denmark did not escape the attention of the media. Prayers were offered for her in many places. Her story was reported on the Lutheran Hour, an international radio broadcast conducted by Dr. Walter A. Maier, one of the most famous preachers of his time. She was asked, "Why are you going?" Betty answered, "I trust in God." Newspaper stories of her trip were printed across the country. One story stated: "While refugees are fleeing from Europe's danger zones, Miss Poulson is packing her bags to fly above the mine-infested Atlantic, through skies thick with war planes, to cast her lot in Europe's uncertain future with her childhood sweetheart."

Another newspaper wrote: "An excited young woman prepared with a light heart Friday to return to her native Denmark, now occupied by Nazi legions of Germany. The bride-to-be was unimpressed by prospects of life under Nazi control. 'Erik told me conditions were not bad in Bindslev. I don't believe any German soldiers are stationed there. I know Erik wouldn't have asked me to come if everything wasn't all right'." She was also interviewed by a Chicago radio station. Another letter came from a listener to a radio station in Georgia which had reported Betty's trip.

Betty awoke early on September 7, 1941, at Inger's house in New York. Her heart was beating with excitement as she left for the airport. The Clipper was fueled. The mechanics had approved the plane for flight. The weather was fair. The flight was scheduled to take off at noon. Love had conquered all.

CHAPTER   1 8

The Clipper Flight To Bermuda

THE PAN AM "DIXIE CLIPPER" took off from the New York harbor at noon on September 9, 1941. Powered by four 1,500 horsepower overhead engines, the giant seaplane slowly began to move away from its moorings for take-off across the water. It created a huge wake as its speed increased. The roar of its engines was deafening. Finally, it lifted off. Betty was on her way to Denmark to marry Erik.

Built in Seattle, the Boeing B-314 was the largest aircraft manufactured in the United States. Its first trans-atlantic passenger flight from New York to Southampton, England, had taken off on June 29, 1939. Its maiden flight had been in June 1938. It began mail service in April 1939 and was flown by a crew of nine.

This aircraft was not like anything you'll find travelling the airways today. It was really a flying boat. It had seating space for sixty passengers and room for fourteen more to sit, read, visit or nap in the lounge. There were sleeping berths for forty people. Small by comparison to the jumbo jets which fly today, it was an engineering marvel for its time. The plane was built with a duralumin frame (a light strong alloy of aluminum, copper, manganese, and magnesium). It weighed 86,000 pounds. Its modern furniture was also constructed of duralumin. The advertised fare to England, via Bermuda, the Azores and Lisbon, was five hundred dollars.

The Dixie Clipper had seven passenger compartments with a deluxe compartment in the rear, complete with bookcase and cocktail table. A major consideration in building this aircraft was weight and soundproofing. Its colors were carefully selected to avoid boredom. Its range was 5,000 miles. There was an overhead observation turret to check its position by the sun and stars. Food was prepared before take off and kept warm in the galley. Passengers were free to spend time in the drawing room or the dining salon. There were also dressing rooms. Meals were served in shifts. As it was loosed from its moorings, crowds would gather to watch the unusual aircraft lift off from the water and disappear into the sky.

After the United States got into World War II and started to ferry troops and equipment to Europe, the Clipper planes were often commandeered by the government. President Roosevelt, Prime Minister Churchill and other high government officials, such as Harry Hopkins, used the Clipper planes to take them to conferences for planning war strategy. After the war, jet planes replaced the Clippers.

Betty settled back for the ride. It was scary, but she would endure the strangeness of air travel. Joyously anticipating meeting Erik in Copenhagen gave her the courage to take the risks of wartime travel. The flight to Bermuda lasted five hours and then the float boat descended into the ocean with a big splash. It was a relief to be down on the water again.

The plane was en route to England and ought to have taken 21 hours with all of its stops. Betty, however, would only fly the Clipper as far as Lisbon, Portugal, and then take land-based planes for the rest of her journey. After a brief stop in Bermuda, the Clipper was scheduled to take off again for the Azores.

The plane did not take off as scheduled. The reason given was that a storm was forecast. What Betty did not know was that because of the wartime conditions, the British Security Coordination (BSC) went through all suspect luggage and mail at Bermuda. Any excuse for a delay in flight could be offered. They were especially looking for shipments of material which could help the enemy's war effort and for intelligence information of Nazi clandestine operations in Latin America. It was discovered that the German military leaders had a plan to capture the Panama Canal and place their bombers in striking distance of American cities. The Hotel Hamilton Princess, one of the oldest and poshest hotels in Bermuda, became the headquarters for Allied secret agents.

The Germans had perfected sending secret microdot messages in diplomatic pouches. Women were employed to open the pouches and envelopes and reseal them without detection. If any of the contents were suspect, they'd photograph them and specialists would examine them. They could scan 200,000 letters during a single stopover and another fifteen thousand could be subjected to clinical tests. The microdots, only the size of a punctuation mark, could contain a whole page of information. A two-hundred-power microscope was required for reading them. The microdot method of communication was not used only by the Nazis. Back in Racine, Wisconsin, the In-Sink-Erator Corporation was able to engrave the Lord's Prayer on a pin head.

Bermuda was a convenient place for planes to refuel with gasoline when crossing the South Atlantic. A part of the West Indies, it's located 570 miles east of Cape Hatteras, North Carolina. Mainly coral formations, it has only fourteen square miles of land surface on the Main Island known as Great Bermuda. It consists of an archipelago of seven main and about 150 smaller islands, twenty percent of which are inhabited. Many of the islands are just groups of rocks. Bermuda is a self-governing British colony.

Betty didn't know it, but she was in the midst of one of England's two most intensive intelligence communities, the other being at Bletchley in London. Betty's belongings were carefully examined. The British wanted to know why she was returning to Denmark, now occupied by the enemy. Was she perhaps carrying secret messages or information sensitive to American security? It was better that Betty didn't know about the goings-on in Bermuda. Because Bermuda had been the scene of so much undercover work during the war, Ian Flemming based some of his James Bond movies there. Betty's innocence of these things was her best defense. Her reward for the unscheduled stopover was a night of rest in a first class hotel.

On To Lisbon

*I*T WAS NIGHT and the giant Dixie Clipper was once again in the skies. This leg of the journey took fourteen hours before Lisbon, Portugal, was reached. There would be one stop in the Azores.

Betty went to her cabin to get some sleep, but she didn't sleep well. The Clipper was tossing about in air pockets. That can be scary, especially if one has never experienced it before. Later, remembering this part of the journey, Betty admitted she was afraid, but added, "I put my trust in God."

Unlike Bermuda, the stop in the Azores for refueling was brief. The Azores have been a part of Portugal since their discovery in 1427. It is an archipelago consisting of nine major islands with a land surface of 868 square miles. Its highest peak reaches to 7,713 feet above sea level. The soil is of volcanic nature. The most recent eruption was in 1957-58. There have also been numerous earthquakes. As Betty looked down on the islands they appeared dreary, black and poor.

The Azores were a rendezvous point for treasure ships during the early exploration of the Americas. During World War

II, air bases and centers of communication between the United States and Europe were developed on the islands. Since 1951, the United States has maintained a NATO air base in the Azores. Before the advent of weather satellites, meteorological data was compiled and transmitted from the Azores to offer information for European weather forecasting.

During the Clipper flight, Betty was scrutinized by the other passengers, who suspected she was a spy. There were only about thirty people on board, mostly women and children. Why, the women asked, was she returning to Denmark to live under the Nazis? Betty supposed that they were returning to their families in England, having been evacuated to America for safety. There was also an English doctor who voiced suspicions.

This called for some quick thinking by Betty. What might she do to persuade them that she was an honorable young woman returning to her homeland to marry the man she loved? Then she remembered the wedding dress she had brought from America. Returning to her cabin, she brought back the dress and veil to show them. That appeared to convince her antagonists.

When Betty arrived in Lisbon, her feet touched European soil for the first time in over four years. It felt good. The ocean was behind. Now it would be flights overland.

The passengers were taken to a hotel. Betty had expected to leave the next day for Madrid. Precious time was passing and she was getting anxious. The hotel and meals were her own expense and she had left New York with just enough to make it to Copenhagen, provided all went well. Every day, someone came to tell them that they should prepare for flight, only to be told a little later, "The plane can't leave today because of air raids."

Betty didn't realize it, but Lisbon was a hotbed of spies. Both the Axis powers and the Allies had their agents sleuthing for information which would aid their cause. Churchill was anxious to keep Portugal neutral.

It was learned that Hitler tried to get an agreement with Spain to allow the German military to pass through their highways to attack Gibraltar from the rear. This would also involve the cooperation of the Portuguese. It was feared in London that, if the war swung decidedly to Germany, the Portuguese might drop their neutrality. The British were negotiating with Portugal for the use of military bases in the Azores. This was patiently and peacefully accomplished. If things had gotten desperate, the British, of course, could easily have seized the Azores. Churchill resisted such ideas.

During her three days in Lisbon, Betty could have visited famous museums and theatres, but her mind was set on getting to Copenhagen. Money was also a concern. Lisbon is an old city, older than Rome. It was founded about 1200 B. C. as a trading station, possibly by the Phoenicians. It bears the marks of many conquerors. There are a few inscribed stones to remember the Roman occupation. The Muslims of North Africa overran the Iberian Peninsula (Spain and Portugal) in the Eighth century and remained for 433 years, until 1147. They remained in Spain until 1492. Walls which they built may still be seen. Even the Viking Normans had their turn to attack Lisbon. Together with many other foreign occupants of the land, they are still visible in the faces of the inhabitants.

There was plenty for Betty to see in Lisbon. Her eye, however, was on the airport. She didn't want to miss her next connection to Denmark. Finally, her flight left Lisbon for Madrid where she stayed at the Palace Hotel. With the help of an elderly Swiss businessman who spoke English, she was able to send a telegram to Erik telling him where she was. The plane left early the next morning for Munich via Lyon in Vichy France.

At Munich, all the luggage was carefully searched. But she had to wait. The plane was commandeered to transport troops. The passengers were refunded some of their money. All of these stops along the way were strange places to Betty. Then the most wonderful thing happened as she waited to board the train for Berlin. She met a very nice family from Sweden with an eight-month-old baby. They were returning home from Canada. It was comforting to speak with people in a language similar to Danish. Once again in her travels, someone turned up to be the angel she needed. They had to wait until night for the train to leave Munich, so they found a restaurant and had a cup of tea. The restaurant was packed with soldiers and the music was very loud.

When they left, the night was pitch black and they had to walk slowly to the train station. They couldn't see anything. The Swedish gentleman said to her, "Speak only Swedish or Danish. Don't say anything in English because it's dangerous here." They boarded the train but couldn't sleep much because the train stopped so many times out in the rural areas. When the train arrived in Berlin, Betty was very tired, but excited because her destination – Denmark – was getting closer.

CHAPTER 20

Overnight In Berlin

THE TRAIN FROM MUNICH TO BERLIN arrived early on the morning of September 12. There had been air raids on Berlin the previous night so Betty was glad that she had been on a train. She regarded it as a miracle. The plane on which she had expected to make the trip was used by the German military to transport troops.

The Germans and the British had been exchanging bombs on their major industrial cities for over a year. The damage was devastating to both countries. The bombing of Berlin had begun over a year before on August 25, 1940. Two nights earlier the German bombers over London went off course and had mistakenly dropped their bombs over the center of the city. The British bombing of German armament factories north of Berlin was a retaliation. Some of the planes went off course and hit Berlin itself. The concentration of anti-aircraft fire was intense, but was strangely ineffective. Not a plane was brought down nor picked up on the searchlights because of the clouds.

No Germans were killed but leaflets were dropped warning the people that "the war which Hitler started will go on, and it will last as long as Hitler does." The people of Berlin were stunned. Herrmann Goering, the commander of the German air force had assured them that this could never happen. The people believed him. Berlin was defended by two rings of anti-aircraft batteries. The British bombers were over the city for three hours. Three nights later they returned and German civilians were killed, the first time it had happened in Berlin.

The Nazi leaders were outraged and ordered the newspapers to print headlines expressing anger: "Cowardly British attack" and "British Air Pirates Over Berlin." They promised revenge. On August 30, 800 German aircraft attacked England, dropping incendiary bombs on London. On the night of September 7-8, 625 German bombers and 648 fighter planes attacked London. They came in successive waves. The assault continued night after night. London was burning. The Battle of Britain was on.

On September 15, two hundred German bombers and six hundred fighter planes headed for London. They were intercepted over the Channel. Two hours later a larger attack group came and was routed. Hitler called off "Operation Sea Lion," his plan to invade England, though the devastating bombs continued to fall. The German Luftwaffe, however, was reaching the point of exhaustion. In the three months ending November 3, Hitler had lost 2,433 aircraft and more than six thousand airmen. His navy had been crippled by losses in the battle for Norway. The German war machine's attention was now directed to the Soviet Union.

In Berlin, Betty was having her troubles, too. She could not get a hotel room, so she accompanied her Swedish friends, whom she had met in Munich, to their hotel, where she posed as their nurse. While at the hotel she was told to report to the

German Counsel to have some papers examined and changed. Betty wondered, "What can be wrong now?" She was to find out the worst. There was no space for her on the plane leaving for Copenhagen the next day. To complicate matters worse, her passport expired the next day. She had to get out of Germany or she would become an illegal alien, subject to imprisonment and who knows what.

The travel agency told Betty to go to the airport as a stand-by. Sometimes there were cancellations. It was a hope, though a slim one. Had she come all the way to Berlin only to find out she could travel no further? What could Erik do? Nothing. She didn't know if he'd be at the airport in Copenhagen even if she could get there. She did, however, have friends in Copenhagen and a number of people she needed to contact with greetings from America. Once more Betty's faith was tested. Would the Lord have led her all this way, through many obstacles, only to forget her now? She remembered again the words of Psalm 103, *"The Lord is merciful and gracious, slow to anger and abounding in steadfast love."* Betty was reassured.

Back in Bindslev, two weeks had gone by since Erik had obtained the newspaper from Captain Langloken telling of Betty's return to Denmark. One morning, Erik received Betty's telegram from Madrid. He decided to leave for Copenhagen immediately, but first he sent a telegram to the airport in Copenhagen for Betty in case she arrived before he could get there. It read that he would be at the main railway station in Copenhagen by noon on Saturday. Then he boarded the train.

The trip to Copenhagen took longer than anticipated. When the train came to Aarhus it stopped. It was nine o'clock. Erik waited in the station until midnight when the police came. They told everybody to get out. Erik, however, was permitted travel to Fredericia in Jutland. There were only German soldiers on it. In the morning he got passage on a mail train which had to make it to the ferry by eight o'clock to cross the Store Belt (Great Belt/a channel between Funen and Zealand) over to Zealand, the island on which Copenhagen is located.

There was another delay. The English had bombed the harbor and laid mines in the water. It was two o'clock before the ferry could move. Erik didn't arrive in Copenhagen until six. He called the airport to find out if a plane had arrived from Germany and was told that one would arrive at seven, but they didn't have the passenger list. Erik's heart beat heavily. The plane was arriving within an hour, but was Betty on it? Had she even arrived in Berlin as expected? Had the bombings of the city spared her? He would know soon. He'd have to hurry. Erik took a taxi to the airport, which cost him a small fortune.

Betty waited patiently at the Berlin Airport. There was nothing she could do but wait. Would some passenger cancel a seat for Copenhagen? It was nearly takeoff time when her name was called. Someone had cancelled. Betty would make it back to Denmark, just in time before her passport expired. Betty was fortunate for another reason. Within less than three months, the United States and Germany would be at war. If she had waited, who knows if she would ever have gotten back to marry Erik.

Arrival In Copenhagen

*F*LYING FROM BERLIN TO COPENHAGEN is a simple thing today. In September 1941 it had its perils. First of all, one could not be certain there would be a flight. It all depended on the war. Second, any plane belonging to the enemy was fair game to be destroyed in the air. Betty's flight to Denmark was loaded with danger.

Hitler's decision to attack the Soviet Union gave the West some respite. Having failed to destroy the English will to survive and their military power, Hitler decided that he could not take the chance of having the Russian forces on his back while waging a war in the west. It was early Sunday morning, June 22, 1941, when "Operation Barbarossa" was unleashed on a massive front, the largest the world had ever seen. It stretched over a thousand miles, from the Black sea in the south to the Gulf of Finland on the north. By the beginning of autumn, Hitler believed Russia was finished. By the end of September he instructed the High Command to prepare to disband forty infantry divisions so that this additional manpower could be utilized by industry. He was already planning for a possible war against the United States when Britain finally fell.

Despite the destruction by British bombers on military targets in Germany, Hitler was confident of victory. The morale of the German people was high and Hitler's personal popularity among the masses was strong. So what harm could there be in allowing a young woman permission to return to marry her sweetheart in Denmark? After all, the Danes were considered to be part of the "master race" of Teutonic people. And besides that, the Danish government appeared to be cooperating with the German occupation forces. Besides that, it would be a message to the world that life in occupied Denmark was normal.

Betty's first reaction to Copenhagen was very sad. It wasn't at all the glamorous city she remembered in 1937. It appeared dark and gloomy. That was not the Copenhagen she had known.

But that all changed when she finally saw Erik. He was the reason she had left security behind in America. Betty was the second one to get off the plane. There he was, the same Erik she hadn't seen for over four years. It was a strange meeting in some ways, because when Betty left Denmark they were just friends. Now when she returned they were engaged!

When they boarded a streetcar, then found the windows covered. It was difficult to know where they were. They found the hotel where someone who knew Erik's father worked. It was called the "High School Home." Fortunately, they were able to obtain two small rooms. What caught their immediate attention was that there were many German officers in the corridors. It gave Betty a scary feeling, like she wasn't really home in Denmark at all. As soon as they had time to be together alone, Erik gave Betty an engagement ring. First they read Psalm 103 which had bonded their faith, *"Bless the Lord, O my soul, and all that is within me, bless his holy name."* Then they read the words of the Apostle Paul about love in 1 Corinthians 13:4-8.

"Love is patient; love is kind;

love is not envious or boastful

or arrogant or rude.

It does not insist on its own way;

it is not irritable or resentful;

it does not rejoice in wrongdoing,

but rejoices in truth.

It bears all things,

believes all things,

hopes all things,

endures all things.

Love never ends."

It was the kind of reunion that they both wanted.

After the initial excitement of their reunion, they remembered that they were hungry. They found their way to a restaurant and ordered a cup of tea and a cheese sandwich. It was Erik's favorite and they still love cheese sandwiches. That should not surprise anyone who has eaten Danish cheese. It's some of the finest on the market even today. It's sold all over the world. Now Betty felt a little more like she was back in Denmark. Walking down the dark streets was spooky. One couldn't help bumping into things and people. Betty now experienced what it was like to live in war time conditions. If it weren't that she and Erik were so much in love and so glad to see each other, it would have been a depressing culture shock. Betty had no regrets about these restrictions. The important thing was that she and Erik had finally been reunited. Other inconveniences she could endure.

One of the restrictions imposed by the German occupation government on the Danes was that they had to have heavy shades over their windows at night. No light must escape. Nothing must be left to chance in case British warplanes were in the air. The slightest light would let them know they were over land and potential targets. There were heavy penalties for violators of the shade rule. The shades were kept on the windows until the war ended. Then they all were removed as a part of their liberation celebration and burned in the streets. Candles were lit and placed in the windows.

Unknown to Erik and Betty, events were moving swiftly which would soon change the world situation. President Roosevelt and Prime Minister Churchill had met just a few weeks before on board the new battleship H. M. S. Prince of Wales near Newfoundland. The meeting included a worship service using the Anglican liturgy. Churchill himself selected the hymns. The British and American flags draped the pulpit. Three months later on December 10 the battleship was sunk by Japanese torpedoes in the South Pacific. It was the pride of the British navy.

Churchill drafted a statement to which Roosevelt agreed that any further encroachments by Japan in the south-west Pacific would produce a situation in which the United States Government would be compelled to take counter-measures, even though these might lead to war between the United States and Japan. They also drew up the Atlantic Charter, setting out a joint Anglo-American commitment to a post-war world in which the rights of all people were to be respected as to what kind of a government they should have. The Charter was incorporated in the Declaration of the United Nations.

This act of optimism took place while Leningrad was under heavy siege and anti-Nazi demonstrations were being crushed in Paris. But a significant change happened on September 14, the first day that Betty and Erik had together in Copenhagen. Marshall Zhukov, the Russian Commander, ordered a counter-attack on the German forces threatening Leningrad. It was successful and Leningrad held fast.

On the day Betty and Erik left for Bindslev, it was not good in the Ukraine. A half a million Soviet troops surrendered to the Germans. Hitler boasted of his conquests of Russia's rich agricultural lands, "We'll supply grain to all in Europe who need it." It was not known yet to the world that the Nazis were murdering Jews wherever they found them in their conquests, even women with nursing children. Their treatment of children is too horrible to describe.

This was the kind of Europe to which Betty was returning. One would suppose that if she were a realist, she'd have played it safe in America and would have written Erik saying, "As soon as the war is over I'll come back and marry you." But her faith was realistic, believing that it was God's will and that ultimately good must triumph over evil. But now they must hurry home to Bindslev. Their families were waiting.

CHAPTER 22

Back Home To Bindslev

THE TRIP BACK TO BINDSLEV ought to have been the most care-free train ride Betty ever took. It started out that way. The journey across Zealand went smoothly until they came to the Store Belt, the body of water which separates Zealand from the island of Fyn (pronounced "Finn"). The British pilots had dropped mines into the water along the ferry lanes. Trains were loaded on the ferry and ordinarily the trip would take only an hour. But with the danger of striking mines, progress slowed considerably. One mine exploding against the heavily-loaded ferry would put an end to all of Betty's dreams. It was scary.

They reached Fyn safely and had easy travel across the island. They were in danger, however, of British bombers all the way. "Will we ever get to Bindslev?" Betty wondered. She had experienced so many threats to her hopes for returning to Denmark to marry Erik. One could not blame her if she felt anxious. Erik had lived through a year and a half of German occupation and war time conditions. This was Betty's first experience in a Denmark in which an enemy ruled. Conditions, however, were not really so dangerous as they would become within two years, when the Germans clamped down on the Danes with martial law.

They made it safely to the peninsula of Jutland on which Bindslev was situated at the very north end. The train ride north is quite scenic. They went through Vejle (pronounced "Vaila"), the home of modern day Legoland where Lego blocks are manufactured. They also went through Aarhus, a beautiful city with a quaint "Old Town." They went through Randers, an area where the Danish Resistance was particularly active.

The next major city through which they travelled was Aalborg, known for its akvavit, a clear Scandinavian liquor flavored with caraway seeds. Here they crossed the Limfjord, a body of water which cuts through the northern tip of Jutland, dividing Vendsyssel from the rest of the peninsula. They continued on past Hjorring to Sindal where they got off. Sindal is about five miles south of Bindslev. The train continued to Frederikshaven on the east coast of Jutland up to the north tip of Jutland to where the Skagerrak and Kattegat seas meet with angry clashes.

The train was late. It should have arrived in Sindal in early evening. It was two o'clock in the morning of September 16 before it finally arrived. This could happen frequently in war time. All of their families were there to meet them. They had kept dinner waiting all that time. It would be the most welcome meal of Betty's life. Betty thought she was in heaven. She was overwhelmed by the sight of so many people who cared for her. Her faith was vindicated. Nothing is impossible for God.

The next few weeks were busy. They had so much planning and work to do. Where would they live when they were married? It turned out that an apartment above the Waehrens

Clothing Store was available to them. It needed some fixing up if a new bride was to live in it. They hired a painter to do the decorating. Since Erik's father didn't work at tailoring any more, Erik had become the first man in the store. His days were filled with long hours, but he worked happily because Betty had arrived safely. There was work for Betty, too, as they had only two months to get ready for their big day. The dream of her life was about to come true. She had never felt so happy in her whole life. For the moment she was blind to Denmark's difficult straits.

It may have seemed to the outside world that Denmark was passively accepting the German occupation. The truth is that the people were seething with resentment and anger at the enemy. On June 5, Denmark's Constitution Day, there was a soccer game (the Europeans call it "football") between Denmark and Sweden. Danish, Swedish, and German flags were flying over the stadium. Everything seemed jovial until the Nazi band started playing martial music and giving their stiff-arm salutes and saying "Heil Hitler." The Danish and Swedish national anthems were played, but the crowed continued singing – "Ja vi elsker dette landet" – the Norwegian national anthem, as a slap at the Germans.

Suddenly an angry Dane turned around and pushed one of the German soldiers. A fight broke out and the whole crowd turned on the Germans with their pent-up emotions. There was punching, kicking and wielding of beer bottles. The police swarmed in and arrested several people, but it was the last international soccer game held during the Occupation. So much for the peaceful coexistence between the Aryan Nordic cousins. The German soldiers became more jittery. One day a soldier bayoneted a twelve-year-old boy who smiled at them as they passed.

Germany's invasion of Russia changed the Resistance movement in Denmark. Prior to June 22, the Communists in Denmark refused to be a part of the Resistance. In fact they appeared pro-Nazi. But after the invasion when many Communists were arrested and sent to German concentration camps, the party went underground. Aksel Larsen, a member of parliament and the chairman of the Danish Communist Party became an active leader against the Nazis. The Communists were the only Danes who were trained at sabotage, so they were welcomed with some caution by the rest of the Danes.

The people also became angry at their government that autumn. The leaders signed the "Anti-Comintern Pact" on November 25, 1941. It was an anti-Communist document also signed by Germany, Italy, Japan, Finland, Bulgaria, Romania, Croatia, and Slovakia. The document was forced on Denmark under the threat that if they didn't, they would be treated as an "enemy" country and lose what freedoms they had. This, however, made Denmark an ally of the Axis. When the people learned what their leaders had done they rose up with fury. Students were the first to react. They went to the Amalienborg castle to show their displeasure, even though they knew that King Christian would never approve such a thing.

A theological student drew up a resolution condemning the leaders, the Germans and the Anti-Comintern Pact. It wasn't that the Danes loved the Communists, but that they hated the Nazis with a burning passion. They needed all the help they could recruit for the Resistance. After a scuffle with police, a crowd led by students marched to the office of the

Danish Nazi newspaper, Faedrelandet," to carry on their protest. As they marched they sang "Ja vi elsker" and displayed the flags of Denmark, Norway, Sweden, Finland, and Iceland. They shouted – "Down with Scavenius (the Prime Minister)! Down with the traitors!"

Such was the state of Denmark when Betty returned for her wedding. Though the main Resistance centered in Copenhagen, its effects were felt throughout the country. It would not be long until the Resistance would affect Betty personally. But now her mind was on the wedding and she was happy.

The Wedding Celebration

NOVEMBER 16, 1941, FINALLY ARRIVED, the day Betty and Erik were to be married. The temperatures were cold all over Europe. It was cold in Denmark, too, but Betty didn't seem to notice it. This was her happy day.

The wedding took place in the Mission House instead of the church. The church was under extensive repair. The work took a whole year. Mission Houses operated independently from the Danish State Church. There was close cooperation, however. The Mission Houses, also called "Prayer Houses," were organized by the laity. Pastors often attended their meetings.

The chief function of the Mission Houses was to support the work of foreign missions. They also reached out to aid the poor. The government did not get involved in this activity. It was strictly a work of the people. The Mission Houses held meetings during the week to study the Scriptures, pray, and plan mission support. They were not a congregations and did not celebrate the sacraments. They were "orthodox" in their teachings and pietistic in their expression of faith. While the church was under repair, the regular congregation worship services were held there. No one would have felt uncomfortable in the Mission House.

Betty and Erik had hoped that the pastor who had confirmed them could also officiate at their wedding. Since he was ill, a younger pastor who was a chaplain did the service. People in America would have thought that their choice of time was unusual. The marriage ceremony was held during the regular worship service, right after the sermon. In the American style, Betty processed up the aisle to the front of the assembly. They wanted the whole congregation to witness their marriage vows. Ordinarily, the public would not have attended the wedding.

A big dinner followed at the home of Erik's parents at five o'clock. Fifty guests came. At eight o'clock, their neighbors and friends celebrated with them at the Y. M. C. A., where open-faced sandwiches, cake and coffee were served. Open-faced sandwiches are a specialty among Danes. They are both a work of art and a delight to taste. One hundred and fifty people gathered to wish them well and showered many beautiful gifts on the newly-married couple. Betty couldn't imagine that so much love would be poured out on them. For the moment, they were the toast of the town.

After the wedding party, they went to their new home above the Waehren's Store. Here they got an ice cold reception – someone had forgotten to build a fire in the stove. Still it was to be their home and they were grateful to be there despite the chilly temperature. All the stressful moments which Betty had experienced in the trip back to Denmark were now forgotten. So was the war. No German soldiers were yet stationed in Bindslev.

But there was a war on and it was being fought with fury. Just four days before, on November 12, the pride of the English navy, the aircraft carrier, the Royal Ark, was sunk by a German submarine twenty miles off the tip of Gibraltar. British bombs were falling with a renewed intensity over German industrial centers, especially Berlin, Cologne and Mannheim.

On the Eastern Front, many German soldiers fell asleep on sentry duty and froze to death. They had planned on a quick victory over Russia and were not equipped for the blasts of Arctic cold which descended on them. The Russian soldiers were better able to withstand the freezing temperatures. On the very day of their wedding, Russian ski troops dressed in white went into action, confounding the invaders. The German mechanized equipment couldn't cope with the cold. Guns would not fire. The Russians were about to begin a major offensive to save Moscow.

Hitler's mad obsession for a "final solution" of the Jewish people was being pushed harder by Himmler and Heydrich. The Jews were mercilessly herded together in front of burial pits, stripped of their clothing in the freezing winds and then murdered. Heydrich would receive his reward the following June when he was ambushed and assassinated in Prague. Hitler took extreme reprisals, murdering innocent civilians.

In North Africa, the British, Australians and New Zealanders, together with other allies from the Empire, staged a counterattack against Rommel and the German lines. Rommel himself was in Rome when the offensive began. He was taken by surprise. The battle for North Africa seesawed back and forth in the desert sands.

Germany had urged Japan to attack Russia from behind to take pressure away from the West. The Japanese telegrammed back their answer: "So sorry." They had plans of their own. They intended, by a swift series of surprise actions, to become the masters of the Pacific. The attack on Pearl Harbor was just three weeks away. To camouflage their intentions they sent two diplomats to Washington to talk peace.

Back in America, the Selective Service had gone into action. Young men were drafted into the Army. Their salary was twenty-five dollars per month plus room board and free travel to places where they had never been before. Many of them chose to enlist in the Navy or the Marine Corps. After completing their Basic or Boot training, they returned home for visits in their sharp uniforms. This put the idea into many seventeen-year-olds to join up and see the world. It looked like an exciting way to get away from the boredom of home and high school. Many took private flying lessons and volunteered for the Army Air Force, including Betty's cousin Robert. Others waited until they were called to arms.

Betty and Erik did not have the luxury of a honeymoon to some warm vacation spot. But they did take two days off to become adjusted to married life. Then it was back to work for Erik in the clothing store. Customers were waiting. Betty had her hands full setting up their apartment and dreaming about her new married state. She enjoyed preparing meals for Erik when he came home for lunch and dinner. In the evenings, they'd talk of their future hopes when the war was over. No one, however, dared to speculate how long it would last. At this time there was no assurance that Great Britain and her allies would dictate the peace. They could only hope.

CHAPTER 24

Life In Occupied Denmark

THE FIRST THING BETTY NOTICED when she got settled into married life in Bindslev was food rationing. This was so unlike the Denmark she had known where there was food enough for everyone. Had she remained in the United States a few months longer, she would have experienced rationing there, too.

One time Betty had gotten some extra stamps for sugar and by accident had thrown them away. The very idea of rationing was new to her. So she went to the mayor of Bindslev explaining what had happened. She felt so badly about it that she cried. She had expected sympathy, but instead he told her, "You can go home and keep on crying." It didn't help that she was the new celebrity recently back from America. This sounded harsh to her, but after thinking it over, she decided, "He had to be fair."

There was always plenty of food for the Germans. It was part of the Occupation's intention to keep the local people hungry. This was done by rationing. They reasoned that this would make it easier to control them. The grocers would like to have sold the food to the Danes, but they were required to sell whatever they had if a German soldier wanted to buy it. Not only was food scarce, but clothing became hard to buy. Many old coats and other garments were made over into new clothes. It angered the Danes to see the German soldiers dressed so warmly while they themselves often froze.

Worse yet, it was difficult to keep their apartment warm. They had a wood-burning stove in which they burned peat. Often the peat was so wet they had to dry it in the oven before putting it into the fire. They also were able to find some small branches in the forest. One day the cream bottle burst in the kitchen. It had frozen. That same day Betty had to wear her husband's overcoat to keep warm while making dinner. One day Erik's uncle came to visit. He had carried a little girl in his arms from the bus. By the time he arrived at Betty's house, the little girl had frozen her hand. It pained her all day. Betty's first winter back in Bindslev was quite a shock after living in the comforts of Racine.

The apartment in which they lived above the clothing store was next to the Danish police station. This actually gave them some security. In the early part of the Occupation, until August 29, 1943, the Danish military and police forces were still intact and were expected to keep the peace. They had to be careful, but sometimes it happened they looked the other way.

On August 29, the German military placed all Denmark under martial law. The Danish military and police forces were ordered to report to the Nazi officials, where they were disarmed and arrested. Many of them refused to report and went "underground." Those who were arrested were shipped to concentration camps in Germany. Now Betty could feel no safety. The Danish police who lived in the Waehrens building escaped into the country to a farm. Their location, of course, was kept secret. The wife of one of the policemen, together with her small child and large dog, continued to live alone next door to Betty. Because they were friends, Betty had some idea what was happening.

Shortly after August 29th, the enemy came to occupy their town. Previous to this, the German military were stationed only on the shore of the North Sea, maintaining their bunkers against a possible British invasion. This was only a few miles from Bindslev. The town's people didn't feel threatened by them at that time. Now they took over the hotel and the mission house. Soldiers patrolled the streets. It was no longer any fun to go out for an evening stroll. The soldiers often stopped people who were out walking and interrogated them.

One night, Erik did not return home to Bindslev when expected. Betty became anxious. Every time he came close to his house, the soldiers told him to turn around. They also searched him. Finally, he found his way back to Bindslev by another road. It was even illegal for groups to gather on the streets and visit. In fact, it became dangerous to recognize friends when meeting on the streets. Deep darkness had descended on Denmark.

There was a sign on the store wall which read "POLICE." The German soldiers would come there thinking that the outlawed Danish police were still in business. One night when it was very dark, Erik took the sign down.

One other night Betty was awakened by noise below their apartment in the store. They suspected thieves. A bank was also located on the ground floor of the building. It would be too dangerous to go down and see what was going on. Erik and Betty started knocking on their apartment window and the thieves took off running. They went down to see what was going on below and found that the office safe was lying on its side halfway out of the store. It turned out to be local hoodlums.

Just three weeks after their wedding, the big news hit. The Japanese bombed Pearl Harbor! America was now involved in the war. But how would that help Denmark? Four days after Pearl Harbor, on Thursday, December 11, Germany and Italy declared war on the United States, as they were bound by treaty to do. That was the best news the Danes had heard since they had been occupied. Even though the United States had supplied fifty old destroyers to the British navy, and had been supplying them with all the help possible while still remaining technically neutral, this was bound to change the course of events. When Betty heard the news that America was now in the war, her heart leaped for joy. "Erik," she shouted, "The Yanks are coming!" Suddenly she became silent and her heart beat faster. She remembered her brothers and her cousins in America. Would they be coming too? Tears began to flow from her eyes.

Sunday evening, December 7, 1941, Churchill received the news that Pearl Harbor had been bombed. He immediately called President Roosevelt for confirmation. The President replied, "It's quite true. They have attacked us at Pearl Harbor. We are all in the same boat now." Churchill replied, "This certainly simplifies things. God be with you." In his war memoirs, Churchill wrote, "Hitler's fate is sealed. Mussolini's fate is sealed. As for the Japanese, they will be ground to powder." Churchill and Britain had been standing alone against the Nazi attack in the West. He later wrote, "No American will think it wrong of me if I proclaim that to have the United

States at our side was to me the greatest joy." Churchill was proud. He wrote: "American blood flows in my veins." His mother, Jennie Jerome, was a noted beauty from New York City.

Back in America, the Japanese attack on Pearl Harbor shocked the nation. President Roosevelt addressed a joint session of Congress on Monday. Many students in American schools listened by radio as he began to speak: "Yesterday, December 7, 1941, a date which will live in infamy, the United States of America was suddenly and deliberately attacked by naval and air forces of the Empire of Japan." When the President asked Congress to declare that "a state of war has existed," they overwhelmingly concurred. The rest is history. America was at war and it would not end until August 1945. Americans were chilled and moved to patriotism. The Danes were cheered and had their hope of freedom renewed.

CHAPTER 25

The Resistance In Denmark

*B*ETTY AND ERIK dearly loved their native land. They waited eagerly for news of Resistance activities. The enemy controlled the media and the movements of the people. "Surely, there are people resisting," Betty said to Erik.

One of the first concerns of patriots when their nation is overrun by an enemy, is to rouse the public to resist. This can be very difficult since the enemy controls the media and the movements of the people. Courage and cleverness have to combine against such overwhelming odds.

Erik was quiet and sad. He tried to reassure Betty, "We Danes are not going to be Hitler's 'caged canary,' as the German leaders say. We do not have the mountains in which to hide like the Norwegians have. We have to hide each other and deceive the enemy. In Norway, the Germans are reluctant to go exploring too far away from their headquarters. When they do, they sometimes don't return. Besides, Norway has a common border with Sweden which the Germans try to block off but there are many escape possibilities.

"If Sweden remains neutral, we can help people to escape to her shores. Many of our Resistance leaders are finding their way to Sweden and then to Britain where they receive training for Resistance work."

Betty knew that Sweden was often criticized in America by both Danes and Norwegians because they did not come to her Scandinavian neighbors' aid. That would have been political and military suicide. By her official neutrality, Sweden contributed greatly to the cause of Denmark and Norway, even though she profited from trade with the Germans. She proved her sympathy to the Allied cause but had to avoid giving Germany an excuse to occupy her land. Sweden had to maintain a pretense of neutrality. The Nazis continually violated Swedish neutrality.

For some time, Erik had been pondering participation in the Resistance. Early in 1944, he asked Betty if she'd agree to his joining the Resistance. Her answer was an unhesitating approval. She said, "Why should we just try to save ourselves and let others die for us?" It was understood, however, that she was to know nothing of his activities. That way the Gestapo could not extract any information from her.

Erik and Betty both knew that he was laying his life on the line for Denmark's freedom. Many times he had to go out at night to a predetermined spot where the English dropped munitions, guns, radios, and other equipment for carrying out sabotage. The Resistance in Denmark was under British command. Secretly coded messages were given by radio instructing when and where the parachute drops were to occur. Sometimes the Resistance learned that Nazi spies had learned about the drops. Then the planes had to be warned to return to England.

When the drops were successful, the Resistance workers had to bring the sabotage equipment quickly to safe storage locations.

These drops could occur as late as three o'clock in the morning. It was hard to work all night with the Resistance and go to work the next morning. Sometimes, when Erik was doing Resistance work, Betty stayed with families who were also in sabotage work. Besides going to the munition drops, Erik had to distribute the underground newspapers. This was equally dangerous. In 1945, Erik and Betty moved to another place and Erik took over the tailor shop from his father. This added extra work to his already busy schedule.

There were problems in organizing the Resistance into an effective force. Erik, as most Danes, was inexperienced at sabotage. They were a peaceful and law abiding people who didn't go around blowing up buildings and tearing up railroad tracks. War was not their idea of having a life. To make it more dangerous, the Germans infiltrated the Resistance efforts. Many Danes were arrested and executed.

Betty and Erik had great love and respect for their king, Christian X. He was a morale booster to the people. Each day he'd ride his horse about the city. People thronged to see and cheer him. He'd greet those whom he recognized in the crowd. Because he was the king, the German officers saluted him. He wouldn't recognize them. On one occasion a German officer informed the king that he had orders to raise the swastika over the castle. The king angrily replied, "If this happens, a Danish soldier will take it down." "The Danish soldier will be shot," the officer warned. "That Danish soldier will be myself," the king replied. The Nazi flag never flew over the castle.

On the king's 72nd birthday on September 26, 1942, Hitler, seeking to improve relations with Denmark, sent him a telegram of congratulations. The king sent a terse reply, "My utmost thanks. Christian Rex (king)." Hitler flew into a rage and demanded that Denmark supply thirty thousand young Danes for the German armed forces. A "get tough" policy was ordered against the Danes. Hitler told his personal agent, Dr. Werner Best, to "rule with an iron hand."

When the German bands put on concerts for the people, the Danes attended and stood with their backs to the band and sang patriotic songs. The concerts eventually ceased. This was part of the "cold shoulder" which the Danes gave their invaders.

The Nazis were constantly irritated by the Danish journalists who used clever puns and sarcasm to harden opposition among the people. The underground newspapers were a highly effective instrument in rousing the people to resist the enemy.

Not all Danes were patriotic. Some collaborated with the enemy. After a while, some of these persons were identified by their appearance. They received additional rations. Consequently, they were fleshier, this angered the Danes who were kept hungry. The collaborators were watched carefully. It happened more than once when it could be proven that they had betrayed a Resistance worker, that they were spirited out of Denmark on a boat to Sweden. It was a one-way ticket but they made only half the trip.

Some Nazi sympathizers were in the Schallburg Corps, a pro-German Danish police group, which terrorized the public. Hitler demanded that Danes be recruited for the Eastern front to fight against Bolshevism. The Germans ran newspaper ads urging Danes to join the war against the Communists, "so that you won't have to fight them in Denmark." About a thousand men joined the "Frikorps Danmark." They were thrown into action on the Russian front south of Leningrad and suffered heavy casualties, including their officers.

There were many Resistance groups. The largest one at the end of the war was known as the "Holger Danske" ("Holger the Dane"), made up of the middle and upper classes. They were named after a mythical hero who came out of solitary when Denmark was in trouble. There is also an old ferry which travels between Oslo and Fredrikshaven by the same name.

Until the American entry into the war against Germany, the Danes didn't have much to cheer about. When the news of Allied victories began to be reported from North Africa, Italy, and on the Eastern Front, the people's determination to resist the enemy became more aggressive.

Sabotage increased in the last year of the war. The Danes became experts at blowing up buildings and destroying railroad bridges and tracks. Germany could no longer move troops from Norway through Denmark to bolster their home defenses. After the railroad tracks became unsafe, they transported the troops by ship from Oslo. The Norwegian Resistance workers cooperated with the Danes to stop the troop movements. One of Norway's most famous war heroes, Max Maxson, blew up many troop transports in the Oslo harbor.

After the war, Denmark built a Resistance Museum in Copenhagen to remind future generations about the cost of their freedom. True heroes don't like to talk about their exploits of heroism. Being a hero is dangerous business. Most heroes want to relegate the past to the past. Erik is like that today. He'd rather talk about more pleasant things, like what a good life he and Betty have had together.

Denmark's Dilemma

THE WAR SEEMED TO GO ON FOREVER. It occupied the minds of the Danish people day and night. The Occupation affected almost every moment of Betty and Erik's life. For the first three years of the war, life in Denmark had a limited degree of freedom, but still the gray cloud of oppression covered the land and disrupted life as they had once known it.

There was an agreement which the Germans forced on the Danes the first day of the Occupation which they accepted "under protest." By the terms of the agreement, they were able to keep their military and police forces intact and continue to keep up much of their daily routine. Hitler didn't expect the war to last long, and in this way, the Danes would be encouraged to join his New Order of the Third Reich (kingdom) which he declared would last a thousand years. (The First Reich, which began with Charlemagne in the year 800, lasted about that long. Hitler's lasted a scant twelve years). That doesn't mean, however, that life was without serious oppression and suffering.

Before the war, Denmark had provided food for twelve million people besides its own population. It had done away with poverty, and had practically done away with tuberculosis and venereal disease. This all changed with the Occupation which the Nazis said was for their "protection." Some people froze to death and others were weakened by not having enough food, clothes, and fuel. Fuel had to be supplemented by briquettes made of sawdust and fallen leaves. Forced deliveries of food to Germany resulted in high prices. Children suffered abnormally from infectious diseases and colds. Tuberculosis returned. The sixty thousand enemy troops brought venereal diseases. Nazi soldiers back from the Russian Front brought lice and the danger of typhus. It was indeed a "New Order," and it brought much hardship to Denmark.

The fishermen formerly had gone far out into the ocean for their daily catch. The cost of oil and tackle raised their costs by several hundred percent. German guards on their boats kept them close to the coasts. The farmers and the fishermen, however, were not without resources. They figured out pretexts for strikes and for not going out to fish. Thirty-five thousand workers were recruited to work in German or Norwegian factories and construction. They were told that they'd be working on reconstruction of cities damaged by the war, but instead were bullied by armed guards while working under poor conditions on fortifications. They'd often work eighty hours a week. Refusal to work meant concentration camps.

Another problem was Denmark's relation to the Soviet Union. This troubled Erik and Betty. Prior to June 22, 1941, when Germany attacked Russia, the Communist Party in Denmark cozied up to the Nazis. After this turn of events, the Russians regarded the Danes as enemies because they had not declared war on Germany. The Soviet government faulted the Danish government for signing the Anti-Comintern Pact forced on them by Hitler. The Danes sent a representative to Moscow to try and get things straightened out. Stalin and his henchmen treated them badly and only grudgingly gave them an audience. Near the end of the war, it was only the intervention of Churchill and the British military forces which headed off the Russian troops in northern Germany to keep them from occupying Denmark. As it was, Stalin had gotten the Allies to agree that the Danish island of Bornholm in the Baltic Sea must surrender to the Soviet forces. The Germans wanted to surrender to the Allies.

The British kept putting pressure on the Danes to blow up German-controlled factories in Denmark and to commit other acts of sabotage. It wasn't that the Danes liked having their factories manufacture supplies for the German war effort, it was rather that this would necessarily result in the death of Danish workers. Among them could be some of Betty and Erik's friends. On September 6, 1942, Christmas Moller, a Danish diplomat in London, broadcasted a radio appeal for Danes to commit more sabotage. He did the broadcast at the request of the British and Americans. Either the Danes must do this sabotage or British bombers would. This would result in many Danish casualties.

The Allies were serious. In January 1943, the British bombed industrial sites in the heart of Copenhagen, damaging the main plant which manufactured diesel engines for German U-boats. Several civilians died. The underground Danish newspapers drew a lesson from the raid and the Resistance was moved to greater action. During August 1943, 220 acts of sabotage were committed, greatly hampering the German war effort. In July 1943, the Holger Danske Resistance group blew up the exhibition hall in Frederiksberg during broad daylight.

In March 1944, the Kino-Palaeet, a major Copenhagen movie theatre, was blown up. It had been a showcase for Nazi films. The Germans waged a heavy propaganda war on the Danish population with movies glorifying Hitler's Third Reich. The Communists blew up a large factory which manufactured replacement parts for German warplanes and heavy weapons on June 6, 1944, D-Day in Normandy.

The Gestapo was the most feared foe threatening the Danish people. They kept files on people whom they were watching and who had been marked for concentration camps or death squads. Their headquarters in Copenhagen was on the ground floor of the Shellhus. The Nazis were cracking down on Resistance leaders, arresting and torturing them, as the war was turning badly against Germany. The British were willing to bomb the building, but the problem was that the top floor housed imprisoned Danish Resistance leaders. Royal Air Force Mosquito bombers carried out the attack and managed to come in at low levels and destroy the Gestapo headquarters. Twenty-seven prisoners escaped unharmed. Nine died. Twenty-six Gestapo staff perished.

A tragedy attended the success. Because of the smoke, some of the pilots miscalculated the target and bombed the French Jeanne d'Arc Catholic School for Children. The school had 482 pupils between the ages of seven and seventeen. When the bombing started, the nuns directed the children to proceed toward shelter areas. Eighty-six children and seventeen adults died instantly.

A successful bombing of the Gestapo headquarters in Aarhus was carried out on October 31, 1944. The attack on the Gestapo headquarters at Aarhus had special relevance to Erik. It's possible that his name was on file there. After the bombing, no one would ever know, since the files were destroyed and a large number of Gestapo officers died in the raid. The Gestapo headquarters in Odense on the island of Fyn was also destroyed.

The heaviest concentration of German firepower was located less than five miles away from Bindslev on the coast of the North Sea. German defenses were fortified with bunkers which can still be seen half buried in the sand. Heavy steel fences, more like walls, were built to resist an Allied invasion. The Danes were worried that their land would be targeted for the Allied invasion of Europe which had been rumored ever since the Americans were drawn into the war. Betty and Erik were fearful for their beloved Bindslev.

BETTY — A STORY OF COURAGE AND LOVE

CHAPTER 27

The Danish People Rescue The Jews

THERE WERE NO JEWS IN BINDSLEV. The people of that northern part of Jutland, however, were well aware of the hostility towards the Jewish people in Nazi occupied countries. Betty's grandmother taught her to include the Jews in her prayers because the world was often hostile to them. Her grandmother said, "We are all human and are all loved by God." There was no anti-Semitism in Bindslev. They could not understand the cruelty exercised against these people.

Jewish people haven't always lived in Denmark. They were first invited by King Christian IV, who reigned 1588-1648. He wanted to modernize the country. He welcomed Sephardic Jews to settle in Denmark. A select group came: medical doctors, mintmasters for coining money, and jewelers. They also lent money to the crown. Sephardic Jews had once lived in Spain. Less wealthy Jews from Central Europe came later. Among them were shopkeepers, merchants, stockbrokers, and dealers in tobacco and textiles. In 1814, the Jews received full and equal status as citizens. The nineteenth century was a prosperous time for Jews in Denmark.

A synagogue was opened in 1833 and schools were established. Many of the Jews were assimilated into the native population through marriage. They lived mainly in Copenhagen. In the early twentieth century, tens of thousands of Jews fled persecutions in Russia, Russian Poland and the Baltic regions. About three thousand came to Denmark. This brought a renewal to the Jewish community and to Yiddish culture. Another wave of refugees came in the 1930s from Germany, Austria and other German occupied areas. In 1939, the Danish Criminal Code provided for fines and imprisonment for anyone guilty of anti-Semitism. The Danish people respected their rights and got alone well with their Jewish neighbors and considered them to be "Danes." No distinction.

There were many prominent Jews in Denmark. Georg Brandes (1832-1927) was a famous writer and literary critic. Niels Bohr (1885-1962) was a Nobel Prize physicist. King Christian had to plead with him to escape to Sweden so the Nazis would not force him to work for them. He felt no danger in Denmark. He went to America to continue his scientific research. Max Henius (d. 1935), whose parents had come from Poland, moved to Chicago after earning a doctorate in Germany. He identified the cause of the typhoid epidemic threatening Chicago in 1892. Henius was a founder of the American "Fourth of July" celebration in Denmark, the largest in the world outside of America. Victor Borge (b. 1909) incurred the wrath of Hitler by his comic remarks about "der Fuehrer." Fortunately, he was in Sweden when the Nazis overran Denmark. He has become one of America's favorite entertainers.

Anti-Semitism did not originate with Hitler. It was well established in Europe. The world had been forewarned about Hitler's views about the Jews. His book, *Mein Kampf*, is filled with anti-Semitic statements. But this did not seem to shock people because Europe had a long history of anti-Semiticism. Many people resonated with Hitler's rhetoric.

The Nazis tolerated the Danish protection of their Jewish citizens to avoid offending Danish public opinion in the early years of the Occupation. They needed the cooperation of the Danes to produce food and military equipment. However, after August 29, 1943, when the German troops attacked the Copenhagen naval base and dismantled both the government and the military, and Home Rule was suspended, the Nazis moved against the Jews. The Chief Rabbi Friediger was arrested. Prior to this, threats against the Jews were protested by the Danish government, but now there was no government.

The crackdown on the Jews was planned for the night of October 1, 1943. The people would be in the synagogue celebrating Rosh Hashanah (the Jewish New Year). It was also the sabbath. The Nazis intended to round up the people quietly so the Danish population would not know what happened. It would have likely succeeded if a German diplomat and shipping expert, George F. Duckwitz, a trusted associate of Dr. Werner Best who was Hitler's plenipotentiary (personal agent), had not warned the Jewish community. Best telegraphed Hitler on September 8, "the time has come to turn our attention to the solution of the Jewish question." Best had been Reinhard Heydrich's deputy and was responsible for the massacre of Jews in Poland and Russia. Both the leaders of German army and navy opposed the move against the Jews. After the war, Best claimed that he had tried to stop the purge. He was sentenced to death for crimes against the people, but the sentence was commuted to five years in prison.

When the Jewish leaders first received the warning, they didn't believe it. But Rabbi Marcus Melchior was persuaded to warn the people at the synagogue services. Of the 7,906 Jews in Denmark (including 686 non-Jewish spouses), 481 were arrested and deported to Theresienstadt, a German concentration camp, where 45,000 Jews were interned. There they joined Rabbi Friediger. Theresienstadt was a holding camp, unlike Auschwitz or Buchenwald, which were "final" camps. Fleas became their constant companions at these prisons. Efforts were made to aid the deportees in Germany, but with limited success.

The Danish people rallied to save the Jewish population. Sweden changed its policy towards refugees and welcomed as many as could get there. Forty-five schools were set up in Sweden for the 1,364 Jewish children. It was perilous work. People were hidden in homes, hospitals and churches. Some were detected and arrested. Lutheran Bishop Fulsang-Damgaard publicly denounced the persecution in a letter read to the congregations. Fleeing from Copenhagen, Rabbi Melchior, together with his family, knocked at the door of Lutheran Pastor Hans Kildeby, forty miles south of the city. He had often stayed there before when traveling. He explained their plight and warned of the dangers of giving them shelter. Kildeby insisted that they take refuge in his house.

Many were hidden under cargos in boats crossing to Sweden. Children often had to be sedated to keep them from crying. Danish organizations, businesses and private individuals contributed money for the cost of bringing refugees to Sweden. The more wealthy Jews paid extra to help those with lesser means. There were some instances in which people took advantage of the Jews, charging them exorbitant fees for passage to Sweden. They were prosecuted after the war.

At the Yad Vashem memorial to the Holocaust victims of World War II in Jerusalem, there is a blue rowboat on display. It was used to transport Danish Jews to safety in Sweden when the Nazis moved against them. It isn't much of a boat in which to cross a large body of water, but boats like these saved many lives. The boat has become a symbol of Denmark's courageous effort to save a significant part of their population from annihilation in October 1943.

Most of the Jews were welcomed back to Denmark after the war. For most part, their abandoned property was left unharmed. There were a few cases in which their apartments were let out to other tenants who didn't want to give them up. Unfortunately, the Nazis had left their infection. The Jews were now looked upon as a separate and visible group by some people, a subtle form of anti-Semitism. Before the war the Jews were considered to be just Danes like all the people in the land. Betty and Erik could not understand this new racism. It had no place in their lives.

CHAPTER 28

The Role Of The Church In Resisting The Nazis

*B*ETTY AND ERIK FOUND THEIR STRENGTH in the church and its teachings. This fellowship of faith had given them the courage to plan their wedding in the midst of war. They depended on the counsel of their pastors and believing friends.

But what could they expect from the church in such trying times as these? Their country was occupied by an enemy who had deceived them and violated their neutrality. The church had only the power of moral persuasion. It had no troops, no guns, no war planes or tanks. In fact, the church's mandate was to be the champion of peace and not war.

To complicate things further, the Lutheran State Church of Denmark, like other Lutheran Churches in Europe, had given unwavering support to state authority since Martin Luther. This unquestioning loyalty assumed that the leaders of the state would be Christian laymen who would take their faith seriously. However wrong the Kaiser had been in attacking Russia and France in World War I, leaders of the church in Germany loyally stood by him.

In America it had been different during the War for Independence. Henry Melchior Muhlenberg, the "patriarch of the Lutheran Church in America," took a strong partisan stand in the war. His oldest son, John, also a pastor, whipped off his robe after concluding a worship service and stood before the congregation in an officer's uniform. He urged members of the congregation to follow him and enlist in the Continental Army. His second son, Frederick, also a pastor, became a congressman and Speaker of the House of Representatives. His statue stands in the Capitol in Washington. The Muhlenbergs broke with the European tradition.

Betty and Erik wondered why so many church leaders in Germany fell for Hitler's propaganda? But the truth is that the Weimar Republic established in Germany after World War I didn't really have a chance to succeed. The Versailles Peace Treaty had imposed heavy reparation fines on Germany. France, especially, wanted to be paid for the damage Germany had done to their country. This caused an economic collapse with runaway inflation. Many leaders of the church were active opponents of the Weimar government and wished for the conditions of the empire under the Kaiser.

Hitler appealed to the national pride of the Germans. They had been world leaders in many areas of industry, the arts, and development of scientific theory. Many church leaders voted for the Nazi party which elected Hitler Chancellor of Germany on January 30, 1933. But soon they were to see a new kind of state – a totalitarian state – which demanded total obedience to the rulers. Totalitarianism placed the state above all other institutions. The church was told that it could only influence the "souls" of people, and that this must not conflict with the state. Betty and Erik totally disagreed with this point of view.

The Nazi ideology was not immediately understood by many people. Even members of the church supported Hitler's National Socialism Party in the beginning. However, if they had taken Hitler's book, *Mein Kampf* seriously, they should have expected Hitler to be a mad egomaniac grasping for power. Before the Occupation, the Danes were at ease and hoping for the best in the land of their big neighbor to the south.

Soon there would be martyrs among church leaders. Denmark's most famous martyr was Kaj Munk, a pastor, poet, and playwright. Several of his plays have been made into movies. Munk had been among those who had formerly admired Hitler and Mussolini. It was only after Denmark was occupied that he saw the demonic in National Socialism. He turned his powerful pen against the Nazi overlords of the country. Munk did not escape their attention. On the evening of January 4, 1944, the Gestapo arrested him. The next morning his body was found in a ditch with a bullet through his head. More than 4,000 people defied Nazi orders and attended his funeral. The people of Bindslev were well acquainted with Munk's opposition to the Third Reich.

There were many church leaders who joined the Resistance. Bishop Fulsang Damgaard of Copenhagen, head of the Danish State Church, had tried to keep communication lines open with the Occupation forces in the hopes that better conditions could be obtained for the people. But when the Gestapo initiated action against the Jews, he condemned their actions and called on all Danish Christians to help their Jewish neighbors escape destruction.

Harald Sandbaek was a rural pastor in Jutland. Earlier he had been a chaplain to six hundred Danish volunteers who had gone to Finland to fight against the Russians. He found the Danes in his parish living "too good a life." German troops were seldom seen. He found it difficult to effectively oppose the Germans except through preaching against the Occupation. Sandbaek joined the Resistance as a member of an arms receiving unit and of an execution squad assigned the task of liquidating informers. He knew he was a marked man.

Sandbaek had been high on the Gestapo's list. They finally arrested and imprisoned him on the top floor of their headquarters in Aarhus. When the English Mosquito bombers hit the Gestapo headquarters in Aarhus on October 31, 1994, he was buried in the debris for five hours. When the Germans dug him out, they didn't realize that he was a prisoner and they brought him to a hospital. From there he escaped to Sweden. When the Danish newspapers reported that he had been killed, the Gestapo assumed he was dead and didn't continue searching for him.

Opposition was mounting to Hitler in Germany. Some of it was within his general staff. The opposition included the educated classes of people, among them were leaders of the church. Pastor Martin Niemoeller, who had commanded a U-boat in World War I, had been enthusiastic about Hitler in the beginning. His "conversion" away from Hitler made him an implacable foe of the regime and it is said that Hitler was shaken after an audience with him. He spent the rest of the war in a concentration camp until rescued by American soldiers at the end of the war. After the war he became an outspoken pacifist.

Dietrich Bonhoeffer, a brilliant intellectual and a pastor, was opposed to the Nazis from the beginning. When he was implicated in the attempt to assassinate Hitler on July 20, 1944, he was imprisoned and hung on April 9, 1945. There were others, too. Near the very end of the war, Professor Helmut Thielicke missed execution by one day because the Nazi communication system broke down. Bishop Otto Dibelius was not only an outspoken antagonist against the Nazis, but took the same position against the Communist government of East Germany after the war. Hans Lilje, who became bishop of Hanover, spent many harrowing years in prison during the war, narrowly escaping both the Allied bombs and the Nazi gallows. Karl Barth, a formidable foe of the Nazis, went into exile in Switzerland. He had been a leader in the "Confessing Church" which opposed Hitler.

The Voice of America broadcasted over one hundred messages to Germany by Professor Paul Tillich of Union Seminary in New York. He was forced to leave Germany early in the Nazi rule for his outspoken criticism of them. He appealed to the Christian conscience of the people to resist National Socialism.

The Nazis orchestrated a movement of "German Christians" which became the tool of Hitler to subvert the church. Many non-cooperating clergy were drafted into the army and sent to the Eastern Front. Many others, both Roman Catholic and Protestant, shared prison cells. It was there that much of the postwar ecumenical movement was born. A common enemy had driven them together.

Erik and Betty couldn't know that so many people had joined the battle to oppose Hitler. It was only after the war that much of this information became known to the public. As for

Betty and Erik, they kept faith with their country and their God. But in the meantime, some new and exciting developments were taking place in their family which would distract attention away from the war.

CHAPTER 29

Welcome Ib And Jane

WHILE THE WINTERS IN EUROPE had been colder than usual, the summers were also hotter. On the night of August 27, 1942, Erik was home with Betty, for they were expecting their first child. In Bindslev, they didn't go to hospitals for birthing. One's beginning was at home, like pioneer days in America. Erik had to fire up the kitchen stove to boil water and the house was smoky from the burning branches. The child was delivered by a midwife. Later, the doctor came and so did Erik's mother, who had ten children herself. She accepted the birth of another child in stride. It was a baby boy, healthy and handsome, and, of course, the pride of his parents. They named him Ib, pronounced "eeb."

Ib received a lot of publicity. A telegram was received from a magazine which wrote a story on his arrival. Betty and Erik had a wonderful time at home in the evenings with their new son. They noticed every movement of his face and hands. They could forget about the war for brief moments with their newly arrived delight.

German soldiers were not yet stationed in Bindslev. But they'd see them in the stores shopping and passing through to their fortifications on the North Sea. It angered the people to see the merchants selling things to the enemy which they needed for themselves.

At this time the Axis Germany and Italy, and their Japanese ally still expected to win the war in a short time. They also expected that the Danes would realize how much wiser it was to be a part of their new world order than to resist it. In their eyes, it was the only reasonable thing to do. And if they didn't, there'd be no choice. They'd just have to get used to it.

Still, it was not a good time to be born. The outcome of the war was uncertain. German submarine warfare was wreaking terrible havoc on Allied shipping. The convoys travelling to Russia to the north of Norway, delivering airplanes, tanks, artillery, and other war material, suffered heavy losses.

The Soviet Union kept calling on the Allies to invade western Europe and open another front against Germany. Stalin used insults and accused the Allies of insincerity. The Allies promised to open another front, but in the meantime there was a war to win in Africa against both Germany and Italy. Logistically, it was not possible to obtain enough transports to carry out such an invasion, but Stalin kept on demanding it.

Many in Denmark feared that such an invasion of the continent would be through their territory. In anticipation of this, the Nazis had constructed powerful fortifications just a few miles from Bindslev. Today, when the shops are closed for the day during the long summer evenings, the people of Bindslev go out to the seashore to watch the sunsets. The remains of the bunkers sinking in the sand remind them of those grim years when they were forbidden to walk on their own beaches.

Betty's family got into the war, too. Her uncle, Hans Kirkegaard, was a contractor. The Nazis wanted him to construct a power plant to be used in case the local power failed. He asked to see the blueprints. After studying them carefully, he agreed to do the job. All went well for several months. Then it happened. The local power failed. So did the power plant which Uncle Hans built. The Nazis came to see him, demanding to know, "Why won't this power plant work?" They suspected he had not built it according to the specifications.

Uncle Hans was a calm sort of person who didn't let the Nazis intimidate him, even though he knew that they could make serious trouble. He asked for the blueprints again. Then he went with them to the bunker in which the gasoline powered generator was located. After examining the situation, he showed them that he had built it exactly according to the specifications. There was one problem. The designers of the bunker had not allowed enough room above the engines for the pistons to move up and down. He pointed this out to them. They asked, "What can be done?" Uncle Hans told them if they would chisel some of the concrete out above the pistons that every one would work. This was ordered.

Not long afterwards, the power again failed, and so did the generators. Uncle Hans knew what the problem was. When he had examined the generators during the previous failure, he noticed that the pistons had rusted stuck. Of course, he did not point that out to the Nazis. Seeing that the pistons were rusted stuck, they again asked what could be done? Because the bunkers were made of reinforced concrete, there was no way to remove the engines and generators. So he advised that they must get a heavy crane to lift up the bunker and then the engine could be replaced. They ordered a crane from Germany.

By the time the war ended, the crane had still not arrived. This was not the only time Uncle Hans pulled one over on the Nazis, and he was not the only one giving trouble to the enemy.

Even though the Nazis forbade the Danes to have radios, they were, nevertheless, kept informed by the British Broadcasting Corporation. Short-wave radio sets were secretly hidden in their homes. They were quick to learn that Mussolini fell from power the last week of July 1943. This created a wave of excitement among the people of Denmark. It signalled to them the prospect of an eventual end to the tyranny of occupation. But the road to victory was not to come easily. As the Nazis suffered reversals, they clamped down harder on the occupied territories. They didn't want anyone to get any ideas of resistance and freedom.

The downfall of Mussolini didn't mean the battle for Italy was won. It simply meant that Germany took over the war. On September 3, the invasion of mainland Italy commenced. Sicily was already in Allied hands.

Hitler was not without hope of victory despite these reversals. He was hoping to revive German fortunes through the tenacity of his soldiers, the disunity of the Allies, and the impact of various untried but novel weapons which included the V-I flying bomb, the V-2 rocket, jet aircraft, and improved submarines.

Even today, many husbands and wives agonize about whether or not it's right to bring children into a world with so much conflict and danger. The "cold war" conditions after World War II and the advent of the Atomic Age also raised questions about parenthood to many couples. Some decide not to have children. Others, with no plan on how to care for them, don't give it a thought. They are simply children of passion. The faith which reunited Erik and Betty together in Denmark for their marriage also gave them the trust and courage to rear a family.

When was there ever a good time to be born? For Ib it was August 27, 1942, because he was born into a family which welcomed him with love and care.

Three years later, on the 14th of May, after the war ended, Ib was joined by a sister, Jane. She was also born at home. It was just ten days after Germany capitulated. Now their family would be complete; they had a son and a daughter. Ib looked like his father and Jane looked like her mother. The Allied victory was a good omen. Ib and Jane would grow up in peace.

V-E Day In Denmark

THE DAY FOR WHICH THE WORLD had been waiting finally arrived – V-E Day – "Victory in Europe." It was May 4, 1945. Betty and Erik were visiting with friends across the street, listening to the radio. They were about to turn it off when the announcer broke in, saying: "We have a special bulletin. Field Marshal Montgomery has just announced that the German troops in Holland, northwest Germany, and Denmark have capitulated." The war was over! They jumped up and didn't really know how to act, they were so happy. Betty ran home where a baby sitter was watching Ib.

Almost before she got to her house, truckloads of German soldiers began driving past their house. The soldiers seemed scared and pointed their guns at the people. It looked dangerous.

When the trucks had finished going through the city, people started singing and speeches were made in the street. One of their friends had secretly made a big sign saying "PEACE." He went into his house to get the sign where he had hidden it. The people helped him to hang it over the street. Flags appeared – British, American, Russian, and Danish.

The next day, May 5, British troops arrived at Kastrup Airport in Copenhagen, flown in by American Dakota transports. There was sporadic and even fierce fighting as the roundup of collaborators began. Four hundred people were killed or wounded in Copenhagen before the collaborators were all arrested. The day was proclaimed "Liberation Day." A sign in the window of one store read: "Closed because of great joy."

About two weeks later, while still in bed from giving birth to Jane, Betty looked out from her bedroom window and watched a little girl give a bouquet of flowers to a British officer. It had been a hard labor and the custom in those days was to stay in bed for an extended time after childbirth.

The last months of the war created special complications in Denmark. As the Allied armies drove into Germany, German refugees came streaming into Denmark. They were frightened and disorganized. Despite their humbled condition, many were arrogant and demanded food and lodging. They pushed their way around, expecting the Danes as an occupied nation to accommodate them. They were furious when they didn't receive the obedient responses which they expected.

Having lived in a country for over ten years where the newspapers and radios were tools of Nazi propaganda, the German refugees were surprised to discover that the Danes weren't the happy cousins they had been told about. They had been taught to believe that the people of Denmark were delighted to be included under the protection of the Third Reich. When their dreams came tumbling down about winning the war and setting up a new world order, the Germans were shocked.

The Danes were astonished to learn of the horrors of the Nazi death camps. It surprised them that nobody in Germany seemed to know anything about those camps and that nobody even belonged to the Nazi party.

A bright light near the end of the war was the return of Scandinavians from Germany – Danish policemen, Jews, and Norwegians imprisoned in Germany. Count Folke Bernadotte of the Swedish Red Cross had arranged with Heinrich Himmler to have them released from the camps and taken to Sweden by a caravan of 94 white buses with red crosses painted on their roofs and sides. Bernadotte knew one of Himmler's weaknesses: he had a deep interest in Scandinavian runic inscriptions. Himmler was emotionally affected and expressed deep gratitude when presented with a seventeenth-century Swedish work on the subject. The gift was considered very special since Germany's fortunes were so low.

Himmler was still a hard Nazi, but Bernadotte persisted and finally won release of the prisoners, as a sign of better relations with Sweden. This was perhaps the only humanitarian deed that Himmler had ever done. He didn't have much time as American troops under Gen. George S. Patton had pushed their way into Czechoslovakia and the Russians were at the outskirts of Berlin. The Netherlands were liberated. Resistance in the Hamburg area was crumbling.

As buses approached the southern border of Denmark in April 1945, the Danish people filled the roadsides, waving Danish flags and shouting "Velkommen til Danmark!" "Welcome to Denmark!" The demonstration was so noisy that the Germans announced over loudspeakers that unless it quieted down the prisoners would be returned to Germany. The people stopped cheering and throwing flowers, but continued to wave their flags. Some of the returning prisoners were smiling, others were crying. All the surviving 4,400 Scandinavian prisoners were returned. The Gestapo guards were glum.

People remarked how well the Danish Jews looked. This was no thanks to the Nazis' care of prisoners, but because their fellow Danes sent them food packages. There was sorrow because fifty-two had died in the concentration camps. The condition of the policemen was not as good. But the Scandinavians were the fortunate ones. Many of the other prisoners in concentration camps were loaded into box cars and shipped to destinations unknown. One of these trains arrived in Denmark with 2,800 non-Scandinavian women, half-naked and crying with hunger.

Once in Denmark they were greeted with food and friendly smiles. They were served hot chocolate, a favorite of the Danes, and tables were laden with bread, butter, and cheeses. The Danes even put white tablecloths on the tables and decorated them with flowers.

Of the 5,975 Danes imprisoned in Germany, there were 562 deaths. Nine thousand Norwegians had been imprisoned in Germany during the war, of whom 1,530 died; but 736 of the 760 Norwegian Jews were killed. Near the end of the war, a Norwegian pastor asked a Nazi official why Germany was willing to save the Scandinavian prisoners. He replied: "It is now time to save the best of the remaining people of Western Europe." The Nazis were racists to the end.

The people of Denmark had expected the war to end when they heard on May 1 of Hitler's death. The next day Berlin fell to the Russians. The first British troops crossed into Denmark at six o'clock on the afternoon of May 5. The German troops laid down their arms without incident.

All Denmark was free, except the island of Bornholm. The Germans wanted to continue the war on the Eastern Front. Asked by the Danes to surrender, they would surrender only to the British, even to a lone British officer. But this was against the Allied agreement with Russia. Russian bombers began their work of destruction. On May 9, the Germans surrendered. Five thousand Russian troops swarmed onto the island where they remained for eleven months. On May 8, British troops arrived in Norway. The war was over in Europe!

Now, Betty and Erik could begin their life anew. This was the first opportunity they had to live their married life under the conditions of peace. Their prayers were being answered. Ib and Jane could learn to know Denmark as it really was.

CHAPTER 31

Return To America

THE WAR WAS OVER. Betty and Erik could now make some plans for living without constantly wondering what new threats from an "evil empire" might smash their hopes.

Denmark was once again in control of its own borders. But the effects of the war were to stay with them a long time. The Nazis had looted the Bank of Denmark. This hurt their national economy. There were many wounds to heal. The Occupation had raised the specter of distrust and suspicion of neighbor against neighbor. Danish girls who fraternized with German soldiers were made into a public spectacle. Many of them had their heads shaved and were paraded through the streets. Even after there was a general amnesty given to those who had been deprived of their civil rights because of collaboration with the Germans, bitterness continued.

German soldiers bought much of the civilian goods which were needed by the Danes and took them home to Germany when they were on leave. However, at the end of the war, while going back to Germany, they were relieved of their extra baggage as they crossed the border. Security was tight. The Danes were looking for those who had committed criminal acts against their country. They were arrested and tried. Trials were held and war criminals were punished. Many committed suicide.

Civilian goods were scarce all over the world. However, when tires became available, Betty's Uncle Martinus in Racine boxed up tires and shipped them to relatives in Denmark. Clothes were also sent from America. Mail could again be sent between the two countries. It was possible to renew acquaintances with family and friends who had been separated for years. Soon travel began again between Denmark and America. To begin with, it was mostly the Danish-Americans who did the travelling.

This renewed communication with America made Betty lonesome for her family in Racine. The war had kept them so busy that they didn't have much time for such sentiments. But now, the ties between them tightened. In 1949, four years after the war ended, Dr. and Mrs. Schneller from Racine paid Betty and Erik a visit. The Schnellers had befriended Betty when she first came to America. Then Betty started to think how nice it would be to go back to Wisconsin. That would have to wait a while, however, since in 1950, they bought their own house. By this time Ib was nine and a half years old and Jane seven. It would be a great experience for them.

Their thoughts were to stay in America for two years. If all went well, maybe a little longer. Erik welcomed a break from doing tailoring work. It had become wearisome. This would give him the opportunity to find a different kind of work in America, something that he might really like. Fortunately, they found someone they trusted to rent their house. But in case America didn't work out, they didn't want to sell it.

They left Denmark on Friday, May 16, 1952, on the Oslofjord, a Norwegian cruise liner. It was Norway's top of the line. The war had been over for seven years and Betty was very lonesome for her mother and family in America. The following day was "Syttende Mai," May 17, when the Norwegians celebrated their Constitution of 1814. There was a lot of excitement on the ship that day. The Norwegians sang their national anthem, "Ja, vi elsker dette landet" ("Yes, we love that land") and other patriotic songs. They danced and feasted on Norway's best food. Wherever groups of Norwegians gather on May 17, they celebrate. Some of them too much.

When they arrived in Racine, Betty immediately got a job at a bakery. Racine is famous for its Danish breads and pastries. Most famous of all is their kringle, a tasty coffee cake available with about thirty different fruit and nut fillings. At one time, Racine was said to be fifty percent Danish. The Danes still make up a significant part of the city's population. However, if you looked at the yellow pages of the phone book you'd think it was a hundred percent Danish. There are about a half a dozen major bakeries with fifteen retail outlets. Thirteen of them headline Danish pastries in their ads.

Erik found work in construction. Even though the American way of life was different from Denmark and the language was sometimes a problem, Erik was at first glad to be in America and made many friends, including his employer who visited them later in Denmark. Racine is a manufacturing city and the building trades are a major part of the economy. It's heavily unionized.

The children got along famously. They went to school and learned English quickly. They made friends and had lots of fun in America. It was a great experience for them.

They were fortunate to find a house owned by an elderly lady who wanted to take a trip to Denmark. But a good deal of their time was spent with their many relatives in Racine. Everybody wanted to visit with them.

Things had not stood still in Denmark since the war ended. The country was busy trying to get back on its feet. There were international issues. One of these was Denmark's admission into the United Nations. Because of their forced signing of the Anti-Comintern Pact, Russia objected to Denmark's admission. They finally withdrew their objections and Denmark became a charter member. Denmark was at first hesitant to become a member of the North Atlantic Treaty Organization (NATO). They were inclined to follow Sweden's non-alignment policy. However, Norway strongly urged them to join and they signed in on April 4, 1949.

Denmark also had some grave territorial problems. The Danes in South Slesvig lived among a German majority and had been a part of Germany for twenty-five years. The German refugees from the Soviet zone, who settled in South Slesvig after the war, would have welcomed incorporation into Denmark. They would then have escaped from the ranks of the defeated and the difficulties of being refugees in the British-controlled area of Germany. The Germans offered to hold an election. The Danes decided to "wait and see." The rapid recovery of West Germany, due to the Marshall Plan, soon quieted the agitation.

The Faero Islands became an issue of Danish sovereignty. Occupied by the British during the war, they were allowed to fly the Danish flag, use their own currency, and had full powers of self-government. After the war, the question of independence came up. By a narrow margin they decided on independence, except in foreign relations. They have a representation in the Danish parliament. Iceland, however, voted for full independence and established a republic with a president, in 1950.

Betty was happy to be reunited with her family in America and would have been satisfied to remain there. The children found the New World a happy place. But she realized that Erik felt a responsibility for his family in Denmark and wanted to return. Denmark was calling him home.

CHAPTER 32

Happy To Be Home Again
– In Denmark

THE TRIP BACK TO DENMARK at the end of January 1953, came during the coldest part of the winter. There was the usual round of farewell parties by Betty's family in Racine. These were emotionally-charged for Betty. She was leaving her mother, sister, brothers, Papa John, and a host of uncles, aunts, and cousins. They all wished Betty and her family well. But there was a reluctance to see them go. Would they ever meet again?

They booked passage in the Swedish liner Stockholm for their return to Denmark. The trip turned out to be a trying experience. Their son, Ib, became very ill with the flu. He had not improved when they had to leave Racine. To complicate matters, they encountered one of those fierce winter storms. The ocean waves on the North Atlantic became so high that nobody could stay on the deck. Then Betty herself became sick. The ship's doctor prescribed penicillin for Ib, but it didn't seem to help much. One day, Erik returned to their cabin and told Betty of an incident on the ship. A passenger, a little too drunk, got in a fight with a waiter and drew his knife. The security officers arrested the man and put him in the ship's detention where he set his mattress on fire. It could have been dangerous to everyone on board.

Betty and Erik were grateful to arrive back in Denmark safely. After arriving, they hurried Ib to a doctor who said, "He is very near to having pneumonia." After medical care, he began to improve and soon was well again.

Erik was never really happy in America. There were times, of course, when he enjoyed seeing sights and meeting Betty's family. But his heart had never left Denmark. Travel was expensive and they had both worked hard to save enough money for the return passage. The tickets had cost them all their cash. When they arrived in Bindslev, they stayed with Erik's parents because their house was still rented out. The renters had promised in writing that as soon as they returned, they would move out so they could occupy their house again. But, somewhere along the way, the letter was lost. So they had difficulty getting back into their own home. It took three months before they could move into their own house.

Getting home to Denmark wasn't all joy. They had to start over again to earn money to live. Erik went back working as a tailor, but had to take work whenever he could find it. Betty was all stressed out from the trip and became hospitalized. It took a while before life became normalized. Nonetheless, Erik was glad to be back in Denmark and Betty was glad to have been with her family in America again. And, of course, Erik's family was glad to have them all back in Denmark.

Denmark was still trying to get back to normal after the trauma of Nazi oppression. The memories of the war were still on everyone's mind. The war was over but the pain remained. Denmark's political scene was fragmented into many parties, none of which could command a majority. The foreign policy of the nation changed after World War II. The Danes would not seek to be neutrals anymore. They had to be counted among those who would stand up for freedom in the world, joining both the United Nations and the North Atlantic Treaty Organization (NATO). For the first time in 150 years, Denmark received a promise of aid in the event of an attack.

The Communist Party in Denmark had always presented problems to the majority of the people. Until 1959, they had been obedient to orders from Moscow. An early enthusiast for Communism was Martin Andersen Nexo (1869-1954), a writer on the literary political left. After his travels in Spain and Italy, he identified himself for the rest of his life with the proletariat and chose to write about the impoverished men and women whom he claimed God had forgotten. He came to equate poverty with innate goodness.

Andersen Nexo came to regard the traditional values of church, state, and home as false, if they led to a disregard of the daily needs of the common person. He looked on Marxism as the way to the Golden Age. His interest was with the material problems of life and he did not concern himself with issues of the "future life." His novel, *Pelle the Conqueror*, is a classic proletarian story of an aged father and his son who experienced oppression from the upper classes. It seems proper that Andersen Nexo moved to East Germany, where he died in 1954.

Denmark depended for its economy on international trade. To remove to trade barriers, Denmark had joined the European Economic Cooperation, a development of the Marshall Plan which later developed into the present Organization for Economic Cooperation and Development. In 1959-60, Denmark participated in the European Free Trade Association. Today, there is a free Nordic labor market, a common passport area, equality of social rights and benefits, and identical legislation in a variety of fields. It comes as a surprise when travelling from one Scandinavian country to another that there is no one who asks for your passport.

King Christian X, the grand monarch who had done so much to keep the Danish morale high during the war, died in 1947, two years after hostilities ceased. He was succeeded by his son, Frederik IX, who was king for twenty-five years until 1972. His wife, Queen Ingrid, was from the royal house of Sweden. Frederik was the first Danish king in three hundred years to have seen active duty in the Danish navy.

In 1953, Denmark amended its constitution, abolishing the "Landsting," the upper chamber of their parliament. That left them only with the "Folketing," the "peoples assembly." Class distinctions were eroding. Another change in the constitution was allowing women to have the right of succession. This enabled Margrethe, Frederik's daughter, to become the Queen after his unexpected death January 14, 1972. She was proclaimed from the balcony of Christiansborg Palace as Margrethe II. Thousands cheered in the palace square and millions watched on television. Her motto is "God's Help – the People's Love – Denmark's Strength."

Erik eventually became a journalist and reported news for the Vendsyssel Tidende (Times). He enjoyed this new work. Now in their early 80s, Betty and Erik enjoy spending most of their time in Bindslev, a town which they love and are loved. Much of their attention is on their family. Jane married a professor who teaches Spanish literature at Duke University in

Durham, North Carolina. They have made frequent trips to Spain, as well as to Denmark. Ib and his wife live at Roskilde, an old and famous city west of Copenhagen, where Danish royalty are buried in the cathedral. Grandchildren now occupy much of Betty and Erik's attention.

Betty has occupied her time with visiting the elderly and other volunteer social work. When reflecting on her life, Betty says, "One has to be some kind of a philosopher to appreciate life. We have had a wonderful life with all of the feelings which life has: Fear, joy, trials, love, sometimes hard times, but mostly good times. I hope to be a helper to our neighbors and to love our neighbors as ourselves. And through it all I have found out that the most satisfying place is to be where God wants you." The church has become an outlet to express her Christian concerns as well as a source of love and courage. Though there have been some very trying times, Betty insists she has never had any regrets about that trip back to Denmark.

One is tempted to write of their lives in Bindslev, "and they lived happily ever after." They would agree. They are happy to be home – in Denmark.